Fail Fast Learn Fast And Move - On

New-Age CIO will replace the CEO

By Krushna Sahoo

Book Creation Services

by

BookMyStory

It's time to tell your story

www.bookmystorypublishing.com

A venture of

R&S Enterprises

FAIL FAST LEARN FAST AND MOVE ON

Krushna Sahoo

Published by Qurate Books Pvt. Ltd.

Published in 2024

ISBN: 978-81-19263-81-3

Qurate Books Pvt. Ltd.
Goa 403523, India
www.qauratebooks.com
Tel: 1800-210-6527, Email: info@quratebooks.com

Table of Contents:

1. About Author

Krushna Sahoo is a successful and influential rising star in the technology industry, with over 25 years of technology experience. He is also an Author, Writer, Public Speaker, and Technology Leader who worked in multiple organizations as a Chief Technology Officer (CTO) and Chief Information Officer (CIO) in India and abroad. The author is a First Time Right (FTR) mindset person. In this book, the author explains how he transformed from FTR to Fail Fast and Learning Fast in a big way, why leaders should Fail Fast, Learn Fast, and Move On in today's world to win big.

He works as a Director of Information Technology at JM Financial Services Ltd, Mumbai. He has written several Articles which are published in various Magazines in India and Abroad. He met the top 300 Industry Technology and

Business Leaders and took their input, which is reflected in this book.

He is a passionate thought leader and has written multiple Articles in Fail Fast, Fast Time Right (FTR), and Customer Experience (CX). He is an Engineering postgraduate in Computer Science and holds numerous industry-recognized certifications, such as PMP and Prince2 Six Sigma Green Belt. He is also an active member of the CIO Club and Project Management Institute.

Who Should Read This Book?

This book is for CIOs, CTOs, CEOs, COOs, CXOs, Business and Technology C-level executives, Managing Directors (MD), Corporate Board Directors, senior and mid-management professionals, and practitioners at all organizational levels, university executive programs, and management students those eager to bring business transformations, Entrepreneur those want to take their business to online model and general readers seeking to understand Fail Fast Approach and apply for success. This book is very practical, and Fail Fast is an excellent approach for success in any field.

2. Overview

A Journey to Experimental Leadership

Five years back, I fell in love with the First Time Right (FTR) approach "**First Time Right (FTR)** "which involves making sure that all the activities are carried out in the right manner and delivering the product or service 100% right the first time, meeting the customer expectation. I strongly believe in this concept and have successfully set this framework to deliver FTR, followed by all across the organization. We have delivered many critical projects with this concept, and this concept creates noise across industries, which is published in various Magazines. Three years back, I changed my mindset and became passionate about this beautiful concept, the "**Fail Fast**" Approach. Before writing this amazing book to share my knowledge with the world, I met the top 300 Technology and Business Leaders; here, I am sharing their input, which is a Game changer for all the New Age Technology Leaders.

To survive in today's economy, leaders must react quickly to market and customer needs. Understanding how technology provides the speed and accuracy needed to influence mission-critical decision-making clears the path for many CIOs to claim the CEO title. While new CEOs may build up this muscle over time, those who come aboard with CIO experience are already primed. This leads to the technique where you must do a quick course correction when something isn't working instead of continuing down the wrong path. This technique is known as "***failing fast.***"

Till a few years back, any failure of decision-making in business was scary & not acceptable. It has caused companies to go off the Fortune 100 list. Blockbuster Nokia, Kodak, and Blackberry are well-known examples of not trying new experiments quickly.

But in the digital era, failure is accepted & it is seen as part and parcel of a successful digital business. Failure must be fast, and the lessons of failure learned should be even faster. It allows businesses to take a shotgun approach to digital transformation.

Fail fast is all about deploying quick pilots and checking the outcome. If it does not work, then drop the concept/idea and move on to a new one. Be prepared to change the pace or direction as necessary.

No business will undergo digital transformation without making any mistakes. Even if an organization has the best possible **culture** & strategy in place, there will be stumbling blocks on the road to success. With digital technologies like the **Cloud**, Big Data, Analytics, **Mobility**, and the **Internet of Things** at their disposal, organizations can test innovative ideas quickly before even reaching out to customers for feedback.

Speed is of the essence here. Testing all the ideas without making huge investments, then delivering the applications in weeks and not months or years to remain competitive. This change has helped organizations to reduce the time-to-market of enhancement of customer experience.

There are several individual examples of failures and successes over time:

- Steve Jobs was fired from the Apple but came back as CEO & made history
- Thomas Edison failed over 10,000 times before the success of the light bulb
- J K Rowling of Harry Potter had lots of failures

- Michael Jordan succeeded after his constant failure to win

There is a beautiful Saying: "If you're not failing now and again, it's a sign you're not doing anything very innovative." Even Albert Einstein said, "A person who never made a mistake never tried anything new."

But organizations don't have this time on their hand. They can learn a lot from these individual's failures but quickly move on and achieve success in Digital Transformation.

This widespread knowledge and strategic business view ready CIOs for the CEO chair with a comprehensive understanding of the ripple effects of each decision on the organization. With this purview, they can make more informed decisions as CEO so that when new strategic thrusts are implemented, they have less overall impact on companion business units.

2.1 From CIO to CEO

A number of former CIOs have become CEOs, including Greg Carmichael of Fifth Third Bank, Stephen Gillett who was CIO of Starbucks and is now CEO of Chronicle, Philip Clarke who was promoted from CIO to CEO of Tesco PLC, and Dawn Lepore who went from CIO of Charles Schwab

Co. to CEO of drugstore.com. Tim Campos, former CIO of Facebook, founded an AI-powered start up, Pulsra.

Indian Firm Angel Broking appointed Silicon Valley Techie Narayan Gangadhar as its new CEO on April 22 - 2021. ViaPlus, a subsidiary of VINCI Highways, announces the appointment of Shreenivas Prabhakararao as CEO of the company's India operations. He was a senior technology leader with over 20 years of international experience in the IT and financial services industries.

As the pace of CIO-to-CEO appointments has increased in recent years, CIOs have become more ambitious. At a recent conference sponsored by **Forbes Magazine**, 70% of CIOs indicated that they hope to grow beyond their current role.

For ambitious CIOs, the CEO job has never been more attainable. The game-changing technologies of social media, mobile apps, and big data analytics have transformed the CIO role from an inward-looking service provider to an outward-looking generator of market insights and critical customer data. In many organizations, CIOs are on the leading edge of innovation and business model development

– giving them experiences that place them in prime positions for CEO positions.

But while CIOs and CTOs are moving into the CEO role at an increasing pace, barriers to promotion remain, most prominently:

1. Many technology executives have little or no P&L experience and a lack of exposure to revenue-producing functions.

2. Insufficient leadership experience: While CIOs and CTOs often participate in important cross-departmental initiatives, some have never led any of these efforts.

3. Lack of success in forging strong relationships and developing leadership credibility among other C-suite executives and board members.

Ambitious CIOs and CTOs can develop the skills and experiences to become effective CEOs.

The CIO-to-CEO career path – once unthinkable or, at best, unlikely – is happening more and more. Wide-scale digital transformation has positioned technology as the centrepiece of companies' revenue-generation strategies, both as the foundation for delivering and servicing products and as the primary touchpoint for customer engagement.

The shift to remote and hybrid work accelerated companies' dependence on technology as a core business strategy and, ultimately, a driver for competitive differentiation. The ongoing changes have cast CIOs on the frontlines of business – not just in a technical capacity, but taking on plus-size leadership roles. According to the **2023 State of the CIO**, CIOs are more involved in leading digital transformation initiatives compared to business leaders **(84%)**, serve as change agents **(85%)**, have revenue responsibilities **(68%)**, and partner closely with the CEO and board of directors **(77%)**.

The expanding remit has elevated the CIO's stature within the organization and delivered a set of leadership skills and experiences more closely aligned with what's required for the CEO.

As IT has evolved to become more business-centric and consumer-facing, the skills that are important for a good CIO overlap with what's required for a good CEO."

According to ***Forbes Insights surveyed 652 CIOs across the globe, 49% of today's CIOs expect to become CEOs by 2025. By 2025,*** CIOs will also play a more significant leadership role in the C-suite. Fifty-nine percent expect to hold a seat on their company's board of directors. Numbers are highest in healthcare (64%) and retail (62%), two industries that are rapidly developing profitable new ways to use customer data.

Over half of CIOs also expect to head a profit centre by 2025. Numbers are highest in the manufacturing sector (64%), where AI and robotics are already used extensively, making it easier to create new products contributing to the bottom line. *As CIOs gain expertise in solving business problems and developing profitable new services across the enterprise,* they're ideal candidates for the top position–CEO. Nearly half (49%) said they expect to become CEO by 2025, a number that's fairly consistent across industries.

One more Survey report, '**The Future for CIOs**: Which way is up?' surveyed 1,000 senior executives from 13 countries across the Asia Pacific, including Australia, China, Hong Kong, India, New Zealand, South Korea, Taiwan, and six members of the Association of Southeast Asian Nations

(ASEAN), reveals that the modern CIO has a strategic role that goes beyond just managing the IT function in nearly 9 out of 10 (89 percent) organizations.

In addition, most respondents (84 percent) agree that the CIO should be involved in all business-critical decisions at an early stage.

"This research shows that CIOs are well-respected by the business, particularly during the past year, when they helped firms cut costs by being more efficient. Looking forward, CIOs need to take the next step and contribute to business growth by developing new products or services and generating revenue," said Neville Vincent, senior vice president, and general manager, Asia Pacific, HDS.

"Nearly 66 percent of respondents believe that the CIO should be a potential candidate for succeeding the CEO - "which shows there are already noticeable cracks in the glass ceiling."

As CIOs harness the power of AI and ML to develop more capable apps and decrease the time to market for new products and services, they will need to grow the skills of their existing teams and find additional top-notch talent. Half expect to play a greater role in human resources over the next few years, which shows CIOs understand that people are the key to harnessing technology to ultimately create the next generation of apps.

CIOs will also forge closer relationships with COOs and CMOs, enabling them to use customer data in ways they never thought possible. Over half expect to play a greater strategic role in sales and marketing.

As a Modern CIO, how do you see the next 5 Years' changes in your Companies:

"Over the next five years, chief information officers (CIOs) will lead their companies toward fundamentally new ways of doing business."

The CIOs of 2025 will be much more heavily invested in business outcomes, with direct responsibility for generating revenue. They will work closely with other leaders to understand how business units make their money and where competitive pressures exist, using their expertise to build solutions specifically aimed at improving top-line results. They will also be rolling out fast-moving technologies, like artificial intelligence (AI) and machine learning (ML), and managing the immense cultural changes accompanying them.

Today's CIOs already hold positions of significant responsibility, and in five years, 66% expect to be critical decision-makers for corporate strategy. Their influence will continue to rise as they become not only technology implementers but also architects of new business models, introducing ideas for business lines and directing changes that will transform enterprises.

As per the **survey undertaken by the Indian respondents**, 80 percent believe that a CIO could become tomorrow's CEO, and 93 percent say that the CIO should have final decision-making authority on all IT expenditures. Indian organizations invest in IT mainly to improve customer satisfaction and organizational agility.

Innovation has been a major driver of revenue growth in almost 3 in 5 companies surveyed. This relationship is expected to continue on an upward trend.

2.2 A New Top Line Focus is Converting IT from Cost Centre to Profit Centre

89% of CIOs expect to have revenue-generating responsibilities. CIOs are going beyond harnessing new technology within the enterprise. As their role evolves, one of their most important responsibilities will be creating new sources of revenue.

"Business equals technology," says David Gledhill, CIO and group head of technology and operations for DBS Bank, a global bank based in Singapore. "My job is not just providing information technology but delivering on business outcomes and customer satisfaction."

According to a new global Forbes Insight Study, Nine in 10 financial services chief information officers (CIOs) expect revenue-generating responsibilities to be part of their jobs by next year.

Cost savings have long been the number-one driver of IT innovation. But that's changing. Across industries, today's CIOs are focusing more on revenue-generating opportunities, as technology is increasingly viewed as a key driver of business growth rather than just a way to squeeze inefficiencies out of operations.

Within one year, 89 percent believe they will have revenue-generating responsibilities in addition to their traditional IT ones. For example, banks can boost existing customer engagement by providing adjacent services to traditional banking products, such as accounts-receivables management and cash-flow analyses to small or mid-sized businesses. Additionally, most financial services firms have immensely rich stores of demographic and customer-purchasing data.

This data can be used for value-added services, and analytics can be converted into crucial new revenue sources and upsell opportunities. In short, the CIOs surveyed expect the technical expertise they develop internally will be useful in the market both to customers and to other financial services companies going through digital transformations.

These executives must master the deployment and management of emerging technologies to identify new business opportunities, take responsibility for introducing new products and services, and become accountable for generating revenue through them. They also must continue to thwart cyber attackers while protecting the privacy and security of customer data and financial records—all while helping drive corporate social responsibility.

CIOs can further drive revenue generation and business growth by following these five steps:

- Take ownership of information;
- Better align IT with business needs;
- Deliver return on IT investment;
- Demonstrate leadership;
- Drive the innovation instead of just contributing to it.

2.3 Overcoming Challenges

Today, Business intelligence (BI), the Internet of Things (IoT), and Artificial intelligence (AI) are the top technical priorities for financial services CIOs. By 2025, ML will become their top critical-for-business technology. More than one-third of financial services CIOs believe that strong partner relationships and using partners' professional services are the most important drivers of technological success.

Financial services CIOs will find they have to grow their expertise, hire third parties to aid them in their innovation efforts, or both. At the same time, they will need to champion the cultural shift to come. IoT, AI, ML, and other technologies are poised to significantly change the way financial services advisors work and interact—with each other and with clients. Some old and new jobs will involve working more with intelligent systems to complete complex tasks. This will require training, collaboration, handholding—and patience. The CIO 2025 survey showed that among financial services organizations, CIOs believe that gaining employee buy-in and collaboration is the single most important aspect of managing a successful technology implementation.

Currently, no off-the-shelf AI, ML, or IoT applications exist. Each system must be custom-built to meet the specific needs of a particular financial services organization. Partners that offer quality solutions and possess deep technical expertise will be significant. By working and collaborating with trusted partners, financial services organizations can explore the potential—and limitations—of leading-edge innovations and come out the other side of digital transformation with high-ROI solutions. More than one-third of financial services CIOs (34 percent) surveyed believe that working closely with technology partners and using partners' professional services are the biggest determinants of a technology project's success.

The combination of AI and IoT will be a powerful one for financial services firms. For example, banks can collect and analyse ATM data from different geographies to determine where to put more kiosks to give customers easier access to services. They can also gain tremendous insights by analysing customers' credit and debit card transactions or tracking who visits branch banks and when to help tailor experiences and provide more personalized services. All of these things will generate new or additional revenues while improving customer experience—a win-win for both clients and financial services firms alike.

3. Fail Fast and Learn Fast Principles and Implementation Techniques

Picture credits: www.google.com

3.1 Business Leaders Must Fail Fast to Succeed at Digital Transformation

"One who fears failure limits his activities. Failure is only the opportunity to more intelligently begin again." - Henry Ford

Why do business leaders need to hurry up and fail before they can move on to succeeding when it comes to digital transformation?

According to McKinsey, the success rate of any transformation is consistently low, with less than 30% succeeding. Even among digitally savvy industries, such as telecoms and media, the success rate of digital transformation doesn't exceed 26%. With such low levels of success, business leaders must reconsider their organization's approach to digital transformation.

To successfully carry out digital transformation, businesses must be agile to rapidly evolve their processes, organization, and the way they engage with customers and react to shifts in the market. To achieve this level of agility, business leaders must implement a fail-fast approach to Succeed Faster, learn quickly, and move on.

Businesses must not be afraid to fail as it will enable them to learn, improve, and eventually get things right, but they must fail quickly and learn the lessons of the failure even faster. To adopt a fail-fast approach to digital transformation, business leaders must ensure they *arm their employees with the right tools and cultivate a culture that encourages employees not to be afraid to experiment and champions learning from mistakes.*

3.2 The Right Tools:

The key to failing fast will be using the right tools. One of the most essential tools a business can have to help them on their digital transformation journeys is data management platforms and customer experience. If leaders are not basing their business decisions on data, they are going to be left behind. From finance to marketing, sales forecasting, and even hiring, organizations today rely on clean, accurate, and comprehensive data from inside and outside the organization to run their businesses.

Data management solutions act as the intelligent core to power a range of transformation initiatives, which is one of a few tactics integral to the process of failing fast. Often, these solutions provide the capabilities to speed up and simplify digital transformation initiatives and can be integral to the process of failing fast.

For example, visualizing data flows and the interactions between processes, components, and people in real time allows for rapid and accurate diagnosis and monitoring of the status of real-time and historical data, integrations, and processes. This means organizations can see the impact of any changes immediately and act accordingly to speed up the process and pinpoint any errors in real-time.

Data management tools will also be integral to setting out new metrics and measurements. ***Technology leaders and CIOs need to set expectations about how many failures are acceptable and how they can measure the success of changes***. This way, it will be easy to spot when developments have failed and ensure they are rolled back as quickly as possible, ready for a new version to be tried. This is something we regularly see with apps and websites such as Amazon, which will roll out tweaks to the user interface to specific customers frequently.

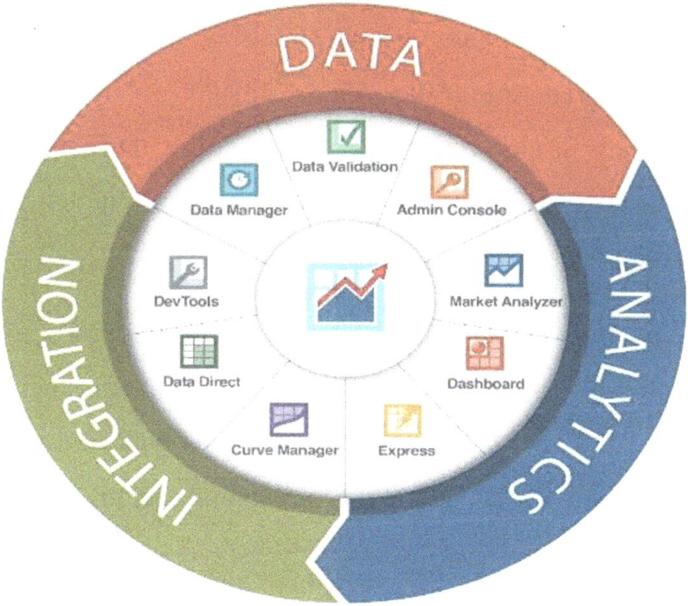

Picture credits: www.google.com

Data Management Platform

"Businesses must not be afraid to fail as it will enable them to learn, improve and eventually get things right, but they must fail quickly and learn the lessons of the failure even faster."

Develop the right culture:

"Creating an atmosphere with no constraints is how we keep our innovation flywheel spinning faster than the competition's."

According to Telstra, focusing solely on technology rather than a broader range of business factors, such as employees, may be hindering the digital transformation of UK businesses. Business leaders must, therefore, ensure they cultivate a culture that ensures that the fail-fast mentality is adopted at all levels.

However, as most people have been programmed to see failure or making mistakes as something to be avoided at all costs, business leaders must lay out clear guidelines of what failing fast means and encourage employees to adopt this approach.

"Business leaders must firstly work to understand their appetite for failure and determine the risks they are willing to take."

To do this successfully, business leaders must first work to understand their appetite for failure and determine the risks they are willing to take. After all, significant risks are likely to mean the organization will either win big or fail big. With new metrics in place, business leaders will be able to better communicate with their employees the amount of failures they expect to see; for example, they may set this at 20%.

Equally, they must also determine what 'good' looks like in different contexts for employees to be able to accurately measure the success of their work and make changes accordingly. Businesses must allow room for employees to experiment and make mistakes as long as those mistakes are quickly learned from and changes are implemented.

By taking a **fail-fast approach**, businesses will be able to rapidly create, launch, or implement the innovation needed for digital transformation, with the potential to completely change the way their organization operates. Business leaders should ensure that all change is incremental - pushing out small changes frequently and measuring their effectiveness.

"If something doesn't work, they must back out quickly, develop measures for how revolutionary to make the next set of changes, and gain a common understanding throughout the business of what 'good' looks like. This will ensure that they are not wasting resources and going down dead-ends."

How does encouraging your team to be experimental with their craft allow them to learn, grow, and develop in the process?

Experimentation is critical to unlocking new opportunities and staying ahead of the curve in an ever-changing industry.

By allowing team members to try new approaches and solve problems in different ways, they can learn from their successes and failures, develop new skills, and grow professionally and personally.

We have an employee who started as an intern and seized opportunities to learn and grow in an extremely technical space. A few years into her Magna career, she became a data scientist supporting Factory of the Future projects by creating machine learning and mathematical models that help everyone from frontline workers to the person driving a vehicle equipped with our innovative automotive systems.

An early pilot project she helped develop used data analysis and sensors to remotely identify, track, and correct manufacturing issues at one of our facilities. The project was a success and is now being used to digitalize a whole factory, saving energy, water, and money.

By giving our team members the freedom to explore and innovate, we can develop new products and technologies to serve our customers better and remain competitive.

3.3 IN THE DIGITAL WORLD, the faster you fail, the sooner you succeed:

How quickly are you turning your failures into success?

Failure is not an outcome; it's a waystation on the learning highway. Too many success-obsessed organizations treat failure as an endpoint rather than a learning experience that provides feedback and knowledge that helps future experiments succeed.

A new study from Northwestern University's Kellogg School entitled "Quantifying dynamics of failure across science, startups and security" found that **"how you fail (and try, try again) determines if you'll eventually succeed.**

Their study documented that what ultimately determines success is what they learned from previous failures and how they applied that knowledge going forward. If they use the lessons to improve future attempts, it will lead to eventual success. If they have too few failed attempts or they fail to incorporate the lessons learned, they will find themselves on a path to permanent failure.

As Dashun Wang, Associate Professor at Kellogg and head of the study, said, "Failing fast isn't just prescriptive; it's diagnostic. If you're not failing faster and faster, you're in stagnation region and not gaining enough feedback to form intelligent improvement."

In a very recent McKinsey Global Survey with 1,290 respondents, two-thirds of those companies pursuing business transformations said that their organizations were just treading water, taking no decisive action, and consequently achieving little or no business impact.

3.4 Learning at the rate of discovery:

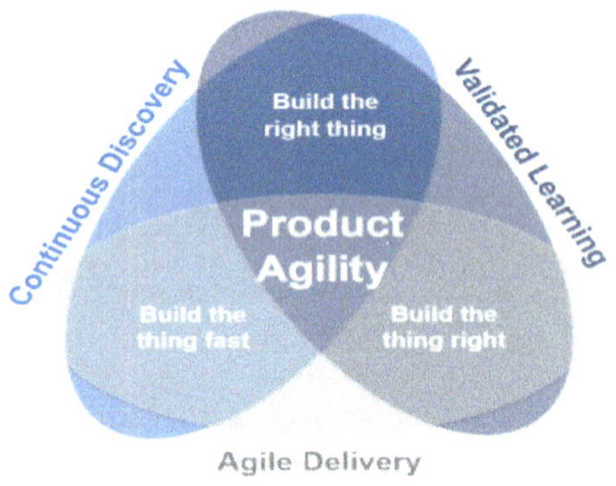

Picture credits: www.google.com

A recent HBR article entitled "**Good Leaders Are Good Learners**" found that leaders in a learning mode benefited by adopting a "**growth mindset**" that allowed them to experiment with alternative strategies and approaches to problems and to use post-mortems to learn from the results of these experiments. This approach allowed these leaders to be more agile in adapting to changing environments as well as to be more innovative in approaching new challenges.

Jeff Bezos has built Amazon around learning on a massive scale via experimentation. As he said, "If you double the number of experiments you do per year, you are going to double your inventiveness."

Speed to market and time to value are the new metrics for competitive success. New product lifecycles have shrunk from years to quarters to months to weeks to days to hours. Those organizations that have successfully adapted to this new cadence are continually distancing themselves from the competition.

Developing and deploying systems of engagement and systems of intelligence enable companies to match their speed of learning to their speed of discovery.

Prioritize progress over perfection:

Picture credits: www.google.com

In the digital world, there is a strong motivation to find the definitive "killer app" that tops the competition. While the goal is admirable, achieving it often takes way too long and thus misses its market opportunity.

By contrast, adopting a **Minimum Viable Product (MVP)** development process allows companies to launch an early version of their offer and get real-time feedback from early users as to what they need to change and add to make it better. The major benefit from an MVP is they learn what they don't know or didn't anticipate their customer's responses would be to the product. This approach allows them to prioritize progress over perfection.

Amazon CEO Jeff Bezos believes that "most decisions should probably be made with somewhere around 70% of the information you wish you had. If you wait for 90%, in most cases, you're probably being slow." He believes the risks of seeking perfection outweigh the risks of making a wrong decision, especially if you can learn from it and quickly respond to real-time customer feedback.

Making good decisions in an era of hyper-adoption and hyper-abandonment:

Good decisions start with good questions. In his recent book, *The Book of Beautiful Questions*, author Warren Berger makes his case for the power and value of good questions. "Having strong questioning skills has always been important. But in a time of exponential change, it's a twenty-first-century survival skill." He goes on to say that "questions enable us to organize our thinking around what we don't know so our discovery process can uncover what we need to know."

Not having all the information you'd like before you decide dramatically increases the fear of failure and puts an even greater premium on asking the right questions upfront. Here are some "courage questions" to overcome the fear of failure from Warren Berger:

- What's the worst that could happen?
- If I did fail, what would be the likely causes?
- How could I recover from that failure?
- What if I succeed - what would that look like?
- How can I take one small step into the breach?

This approach allows leadership teams to communicate the options/choices the company will pursue and not pursue and explain why. It also enables the company to focus on what it's good at and cut back on the rest.

There is no playbook that you can study that provides the right answers to all the unknowable outcomes of the current age of digital disruption. As such, learning faster than the competition is the only sustainable competitive advantage.

This requires that CEOs and their senior leadership teams embrace and endorse the value of failing fast to succeed sooner. These are the leadership skills and capabilities that will determine which companies succeed and which companies fail.

3.5 Underlying Concepts/Principles of Fail Fast

To perform this strategy, one must remove all of the methods that do not work and find the one that does.

To put it simply, "fail quickly and fail often" indicates that the quicker you fail, the faster you will succeed.

In this perspective, failing is the only method to learn and realize the flaws of a certain project before implementing them on a vast scale.

The basic ideas behind the "fail fast, fail often" strategy:

The "fail fast, fail often" strategy observes four significant principles:

Principle #1: Fail early

The earlier you fail, the sooner you can learn how to create something beneficial for your target audience.

Through this, you can obtain real-time feedback on what works and what doesn't.

Then, you can use that to enhance, improve, adjust, and tweak all the necessary areas of the project before deploying it again for testing.

Principle #2: Fail quickly

Failing quickly and learning from it means being able to resolve issues and achieve top-notch quality fast.

When an idea immediately fails, feedback is gained right after.

Rectifications and upgrades are applied, and the project can then be submitted for another round of testing and quick feedback until the desired quality or output is achieved.

Principle #3: Fail frequently

Failing frequently means more chances of pushing the project into its proper path.

The more you persevere, experiment, and figure out which way to go, the more you can block out erroneous directions and avoid wasting time and resources on something that will not end up advantageous for your business in any way.

Principle #4: Fail better

With numerous and early failures, all that is required is to maximize learning chances and transform them into outputs.

One option is to be present with the actual user as they test the project, and another is to code up what we understand as rapidly as possible to help us find the proper route as quickly as possible.

3.6 Lower the cost of failure with proper analysis and find the real problem:

Failure can cost you your resources, particularly money and time.

When you reduce any of these expenses, you improve the likelihood of innovation. One method is to develop physical or digital models for prototyping.

If you want to lower the cost of failure, analyse and find the real problem. Put in place tools and processes to ensure business continuity in the case of a breakdown.

Then, ensure that you can simply, swiftly, and consistently transfer everything from development to production. Then, verify that there is sufficient supervision and reports in place to swiftly alert the team if issues arise in the execution phase.

Finally, ensure that there are tools in place to quickly roll back releases should an error occur by then.

Learning the Manchester Model

The Manchester model applies the 'fail fast, learn fast' method as it includes a science supply chain that connects academia and business end-users. It is essential to consider that this model does not always imply a seamless movement from experiments to market.

A project may experience delays and hiccups at any given moment and must recalculate its efforts while the issue is kept down and examined afresh.

With the Manchester paradigm, companies can accelerate science-to-product innovation by responding swiftly to failure.

As a result, failure is nothing to be afraid of – provided it is managed properly.

Committing to a fail-fast, fail-often innovation culture

The "fail fast, fail often" culture deals with accepting setbacks to generate a cycle of feedback and learning.

This mentality of trying, anticipating failures, and being equipped to cope with and gain knowledge from errors leads to innovation. Success can come from failure, and cultivating a culture of failure readiness and acceptance will culminate in a more innovative organization.

Failures that happen as a consequence of taking innovation ventures should not be penalized but instead commended and learned from. If you want to innovate, you have to take risks.

To take risks, you must understand how vital failing is for innovation success.

3.7 "Fail Fast" to Succeed More in Bigdata/ AI/ Analytics / Data Science:

How is tech transforming businesses?

Predicting the future is always challenging; if you ask me, robots are deployed throughout offices, automating the tasks previously performed by human professionals. Cloud computing, data analytics, and AI have made a significant impact on diverse industries and businesses.

The major challenges now are organizations face the challenge of managing hybrid workforces, controlling costs, and enhancing service quality and delivery, all while navigating complex security threats.

The importance of IT-business alignment:

CIOs and enterprise leaders, bridging the gap between IT and business objectives has become a top priority. But simply aligning these two aspects is not enough. To achieve a meaningful growth, businesses must recognize the importance of cultural transformation within their organization. This means prioritizing key areas that form the foundation for success.

"In my company, we have implemented specific measures for conducting experiments. While it's possible that four out of six or seven experiments may fail, achieving at least two successful ones can provide a definite return on investment (ROI). This is how we are making significant progress. Our main objective is to reduce the total cost of ownership (TCO) for any IT or digital initiative. ***"Fail Fast"*** *is crucial to success; as a leader, you must keep your experiment on, which should be part of your journey.*

Readiness to shift toward technology-based management:

Experts predict a transformative shift in business operations as reliance on human intervention gives way to adopting AI and machine learning (ML) for process automation. The goal is to deliver exceptional user experiences surpassing traditional methods. Advanced AI systems have revolutionized various aspects of business, from demand forecasting and autonomous operations to customer query handling and content generation.

One remarkable example of this transformation is the rise of chatbots, voice assistants, and virtual assistants.

These ground-breaking innovations enable organizations to establish seamless interactions with customers. Forward-thinking businesses are integrating advanced AI capabilities into their chatbots, empowering them to address customer concerns, handle complex inquiries, and provide sophisticated responses. ChatGPT is a prime example, serving as a virtual assistant for scholars, researchers, communications teams, and news agencies.

Central to this strategy is the critical need for a robust data strategy. Without a strong data strategy in place, the true potential of AI and ML remains untapped.

"This is where technologies like low-code and no-code platforms will play a crucial role. They will accelerate the

speed at which business applications are created and deployed while ensuring their maintainability. "

How consumers interact with businesses, how they consume products and services, and how they provide feedback and communicate about them will all undergo significant changes. These changes are made possible by the new technology backbone that is emerging.

Developing new-age skillsets

The core of digitization lies in driving business growth through increased revenue and reduced costs. To achieve this goal, enterprises have to embrace digitization and artificial intelligence (AI) as they continue to advance. *"AI is poised to revolutionize businesses.*

To fully leverage the potential of digitization, investing in data science and data scientists is crucial. Their expertise enables the implementation of AI and unlocks valuable insights that drive business growth.

Businesses and their CIOs face a continuous challenge to ensure the trustworthiness of their operations due to the massive amount of data generated internally by employees and externally by customers.

The advent of 5G technology and its associated computing capabilities will be instrumental in enhancing connectivity and enabling seamless operations. However, as with any business, security remains a significant challenge. Threats weakest link.

We've fundamentally changed our operating model. We've moved to what we call the modern operating model, which was done in parallel to the next-generation technology.

Fundamentally, the business reorganized how they worked with technologies to deliver new capabilities. And we're still maturing that. We're certainly not there yet, but we've made significant strides in the right direction.

Developments in Big Data and AI are having an impact that is reshaping how we think about and engage data and is reaching all corners of business and society.

Companies like Amazon, Google, eBay, Facebook, Uber, and Airbnb are rooted in data and analytics and have leveraged new data-driven business models to disrupt and transform traditional industries such as retail, media, and travel. For innovative firms such as these, data brings speed, agility, and the ability to fail fast, learn from experience, and execute smarter.

Data is also transforming traditional businesses across many industries. From industrial systems to financial services, from media to healthcare delivery, from drug discovery to government services, and national security to professional sports, data is driving critical decision-making. The opportunity to deploy data and analytics has accelerated the speed at which companies can enter new markets,

We know the power of "continuous learning" or "continuous improvement" in anything and everything that we do. When it comes to Analytics and Data Science, I feel it is even more relevant and applicable. The key to success is the model of "Fail fast, Fail cheap" and learn from mistakes quickly.

The only way a baby learns to walk is by falling. The only way we try to hit a "bull's eye" is by continuously trying to hit the arrow closer to the centre. Over and over and over again. We, humans, are programmed to learn through failure; we do condition ourselves to run from risk and plan to mitigate that as well. At the same time, failure is a necessary ingredient for innovation.

1. Data Science demands innovation and an attitude towards it.

2. Innovation demands risk-taking and experimentation abilities, which have a high likelihood of failure.

3. Embracing these approaches and thus failure quickly creates the opportunity to accelerate success.

In the Analytics and Data Science world, we deal with data, try to explore and understand it, try to understand what the objective and what questions/insights can help answer business problems, what different types of experiments can be explored, which would be more relevant, appropriate, accurate, etc. and help business get decisions either effectively or quickly or both.

When we fail fast and fail cheap, these experiments are smaller in both time and money. There are multiple paths and approaches explored, thus giving way to success in a relatively quicker way.

I feel these are increasingly appropriate because we are experiencing it more and more in Analytics / Data Science projects. Some key thoughts are below:

1. Proof of Concept / Proof of technology - or we may call it Proof of Approach, which is trying to accomplish something quickly and "scale" it further for the most viable product development or any larger product demonstration.

2. Multiple experiments during model building – is something where we try and explore different algorithms to see which one works better and has a better outcome as per "actual" expectation.

3. Assumptions – can always be assumptions; however, they can be tweaked/updated over a period as we go along and in a "continuous manner." We need to start by understanding the results we need to achieve, re-strategize our assumptions, and work with business to accomplish the same.

4. Stepwise approach/building block approach in Data Science – we typically gather all information into one system and analyse it by doing experiments. Because, for any organization and its business, we need to understand what portion of it is "relevant" and then refine it as we progress. A lot of experiments are needed in this case.

5. Historical data – understanding the amount of historical data available and developing your analytical capabilities save time and money.

6. Quality of data – If we think we can fix these issues later, that's inappropriate in a Data Science scenario. When we understand what information is key to decision-making and what standardization and pre-processing logic are to be done to analyse data in a meaningful way, we have to do it NOW and try multiple approaches by failing fast. Then we are AHEAD in the game already than our competition.

7. Stop chasing perfection from step 1 – we need to accept it as a fact in analytics and data science and start the "continuous learning" pathway.

At a ground level, the "fail fast, fail cheap" model propels the top 5 trends that are getting more prominent. On the lighter side, it seems to follow the first five letters of the alphabet series (A-B-C-D-E).

A – Analytics, more importantly, predictive analytics...more businesses are leveraging prediction analytics and forecasting approaches to get arms and ammunition!

B – Big data platforms: a more significant number of organizations are adopting Hadoop and Spark big data platforms

C - Conversational interfaces and Chatbots: the movement towards conversational interfaces and chatbots are getting accelerated

D - Deep learning: Deep learning technology is getting mainstream

[it has already gotten attention over the past few years. Noticeable outcomes are accomplished for many applications such as machine translation, different forms of language processing, object classification & detection in images, facial recognition, automatic game playing, pattern recognition, and more. Deep learning is also being adopted because of more computing power and accessibility of technology thanks to various open-source frameworks such as TensorFlow, deeplearning4j, etc., which can be experimented with at a lower cost to achieve the most appropriate approach quickly through various algorithms]

E - Enhanced Data Security: The need for more robust data security is rising, as always

[The increasing number of cyber-attacks and such similar incidents are the point of rising attention to the question of data security. Security analytics may demand a lot of experiments to enable us to get answers to some critical problems to save time and money for organizations and society at large. One of the recent trends in security analytics is increased usage of machine learning algorithms, including deep learning for anomalies and other fields of data science security across multiple industries]

We knew "Data is the new oil." Andrew Ng has mentioned, "AI is the new electricity."

1. *Automated Machine Learning will be the "new normal"*: With more focus on data preparations, data transformations, and data management, the automation of Machine Learning and its democratization of it will start getting mainstream. The framework and life cycle of Machine Learning is always being defined as part of the transformation journey.

2. *Practical, real-life use cases increase and go in-depth*: According to Gartner, 59 percent of organizations are still building their enterprise AI strategies, while the remaining 41 percent of the organizations have already made the plunge. Organizations are getting "mature" to solve their real-life problems.

3. *Innovation around Machine Learning / Data Science will accelerate*: There is no disagreement that innovation in the world of Machine Learning and Deep Learning has accelerated in the last few years and is not new. However, at the same time, despite all new research acceleration of innovation, the fact remains that most of the firms struggle to use these cutting-edge solutions and approaches in real-life applications. This will probably change in 2018 as innovation around Machine Learning catches up with the theoretical research and approaches.

4. *Hardware will continue to augment*: With a focus on Deep Learning becoming more important, the availability of requisite hardware to augment the power of analytics will be felt. Since the availability and analysis of unstructured content, behavioural content, etc., are getting more important, Machine Learning will take a step forward from its contemporary scope of implementation to find additional capabilities for mainstream business needs.

5. *Chatbots / Digital Assistants getting smarter*: Chatbots are already creating a significant impact. Whether it's Amazon's

Alexa, Google Assistant, Microsoft's Co-Pilot, or others, conversational systems are having some sort of purposeful interactions with humans through text or speech. As the plethora of data is being used to train these interfaces, it is getting more important to learn from these experiences by these systems. Chart GPT, Generative AI implementation is critical for customer analytics and conversation.

AI and its sub-components, such as Machine Learning, Deep Learning, and Natural Language Processing, are being used heavily around various analytics strategies for functions involving Sales, Marketing, and operations, thus enabling the decision-making process better and faster.

Major Tech Transformations Predicted:

Global data creation is projected to grow to more than 180 zettabytes by 2025, up from 64.2 zettabytes in 2020. *

By 2023, 70 percent of companies will employ hybrid or multi-cloud management technologies, tools, and processes. * *

By 2024, more than 50 percent of user interactions will be augmented by AI-driven speech, written word, or computer-vision algorithms. * *

By 2024, 5G will deliver network speeds that are approximately ten times faster than the current speeds on 4G LTE networks.

By 2025, 50 billion devices will be connected to the Industrial Internet of Things (IIoT). * *

The global metaverse revenue opportunity could approach $800 billion in 2024, up from about $500 billion in 2020. * * *

Low Code Development Platform Market Size is projected to reach USD 148.5 Billion by 2030, growing at a CAGR of 27.8%* * * *

4. Why CIO & IT leaders will be game changers for Business TRANSFORMATION?

The digital revolution has also unveiled opportunities for the CIO to step up into the role of CEO. Setting the technology strategy and overall direction is a crucial part of the CIO's role. As every company is slowly becoming a tech company through digital transformation, the CIO is in a great position to influence the future direction of the company at the CEO level.

The CIO, with their skills and experience in IT, has an abundance of knowledge to bring to businesses looking to digitize. Operation excellence is parred for the course for any good CIO, and the ability to organize and set procedures that guarantee service delivery are highly transferable skills valuable in the CEO role.

It is often said that the technology sector is the most challenging market to attract, hire, and retain top talent. If the CIO has already had success building a solid and talented IT team, they can translate that to the entirety of the business.

CIOs remain consumed with core modernization and transformation, yet their maturing leadership role wields an impact beyond IT. Recent economic and geopolitical challenges have prompted organizations across most industries to prioritize cost management and performance optimization. Both dynamics have kept CIOs' focus on operations even while their leadership role expands in preparation for the next wave of digital innovation.

4.1 What CIOs Say as per Recent Surveys at the Global Level?

CIOs are balancing the persistent focus on transformation and modernization with a maturing leadership role, embracing responsibilities outside of the traditional IT domain and cementing status as a valued and strategic partner to the business. According to the 2023 State of the CIO survey of 837 IT leaders and 201 lines of business (LOB) participants, functional and transformational activities consumed the bulk of IT leaders' time this year, much the same as in 2022.

The majority of those surveyed (38%) viewed themselves as transformational CIOs, while 26% said they were strategic, and 36% identified as functional. In comparison, 2022 State of the CIO respondents were more evenly split in how they characterized their roles.

Impact of pandemic-era shift:

Even with the pandemic-era shift to remote and hybrid work and new digital experiences well underway, IT organizations remain heavily immersed in modernization efforts to streamline operations, transform the existing IT estate, and sync technology initiatives with core business goals. The years-long cycle of accelerated digital transformation has demanded active oversight by technology leaders to ensure investments are delivered as intended. Recent economic and geopolitical challenges have prompted organizations across most industries to prioritize cost management and performance optimization. Both dynamics have kept CIOs' focus on operations even while their leadership role expands in preparation for the next wave of digital innovation.

CIO's top priorities for IT in 2023

1. Strengthen IT and business collaboration

2. Upgrade IT and data security to reduce corporate risk

3. Improve the customer experience

This year's CEO mandate also skews in Favor of functional and transformational work. Almost a third (30%) of respondents said their CEOs had tasked them with strengthening IT and business collaboration, and 29% cited a need to upgrade IT and data security to reduce corporate risk. Following these initiatives, close to a quarter (24%) say their CEO has tasked them with improving the customer experience and leading digital business and digital transformation (23%) over the year, 84% of IT leaders devoted time to basic functional tasks, most significantly security management (47%), improving IT operations and systems performance (40%), and cost control and expense management (28%).

Security was a higher priority for CIOs in the education (57%) and manufacturing (54%) sectors and those in the manufacturing space were also more committed to up-levelling IT operations and systems performance (51%).

4.2 Future CIO Role:

The transformation aspects of the CIO role remained front and centre, with 83% of IT leaders focusing their time on these types of initiatives. Modernizing infrastructure and applications continues to be a top priority, although less so this year (35%) compared to the 40% who flagged it in the 2022 State of the CIO research. As with last year, CIOs were swept up, aligning IT initiatives with business goals (38%), cultivating the IT/ business partnership (31%), and directing change efforts (28%)—all pointing to IT executives' maturing leadership status.

This was another year where IT leaders were able to spend less time on business strategist responsibilities (61%), which was about the same as in 2022. The high-tech sector (78%) and financial services (67%) were the key exceptions, with IT leaders citing activities like driving business innovation, developing and refining business strategy, and identifying opportunities for competitive differentiation as central to their core charter.

Balancing between business innovation and operational excellence:

Much like in prior years, IT leaders are still struggling to find an equilibrium between business innovation and operational excellence—a balancing act highlighted by 74% of survey respondents, higher among those in manufacturing (80%), retail (80%), and government (78%), and at enterprise organizations (more than 1,000 employees - 77%). Looking ahead, the pendulum is set to swing back to CIO involvement in business strategist activities. Almost three-quarters (71%) of respondents to this year's survey expect to devote a higher percentage of time to business strategist work three years out. They plan to focus on driving business innovation, developing and refining business strategy, and identifying opportunities for competition.

Activities CIOs plan to focus on in the next three years:

1. **Driving business innovation**
2. **Redesigning business processes**
3. **Modernizing infrastructure and apps**

- CIOs are currently focusing on & plan to spend more time on technology and business initiatives that will drive IT investment.
- How the CIO role is changing & where they expect their involvement in other business areas to increase the organization's revenue.
- The reasons for technology budget increases and the skill sets that CIOs anticipate hiring targeting short-term and long-term business strategy.

While it's clear from the research that all companies will feel the effects of these changes to some extent, Innovation Accelerators will see massive change over the next three years, particularly in how they engage with and learn about customers. Their commitment to technology-driven business innovation starts at the top, with the CEO

CIO may also have to merge job roles or create new hierarchies and reporting relationships, "For example, an organization may have to merge the technology and operations teams and reorganize the reporting structures to align the business divisions and technology leadership better."

A strategic resource for the business:

The focus on IT transformation hasn't diluted demand for CIO leadership but rather enhanced their stature as strategic advisors and consulting resources. More than half of respondents (55%) to the 2023 State of the CIO said they proactively identify business opportunities and make recommendations regarding technology and provider selections, while 23% said they evaluate and advise on business needs, technology choices, and providers. Less than 10% said they serve as a risk assessor or autonomous player when it comes to technology procurement decisions. Line of business (LOB) respondents were pretty much in lockstep with that assessment of the CIO role: thirty-eight percent saw the top IT executive as a strategic advisor and 25% as a valued consultant.

The CIO job continues to be more digital and innovation-focused—a trend cited by 85% of IT leaders and nearly three-quarters (74%) of LOB respondents involved in this year's research. Eighty-four percent of IT respondents maintain CIOs are more involved in leading digital transformation initiatives compared to business leaders, and 72% of LOB participants agree. Organizations have come to view the CIO role through the lens of a changemaker, cited by 85% of this year's IT leaders.

Most LOB respondents recognize the CIOs' transformative capacity, but at 64%, the numbers are significantly lower than how technology leaders frame their contribution. Nevertheless, the CIO role has been elevated exponentially during the height of the pandemic and continues today, fuelled by ongoing economic uncertainty. Seventy-seven percent of IT leaders believe their role has been amplified due to the current state of the economy and expect the heightened visibility to continue; 68% of their LOB counterparts agree.

Consolidated View:

- 85% of CIOs say that their role is becoming more digital and innovation-focused
- 85% of CIOs say they are becoming a changemaker, increasingly leading business and technology initiative
- 77% of CIOs say their role has been elevated due to the current state of the economy and expect this visibility within the organization to continue
- 68% of CIOs say that the creation of revenue-generating initiatives is among their job responsibilities

4.3 CIO Direct Line to Support CEO:

CIOs also continue to have strong ties with other influencers in the company. Seventy-seven percent of those surveyed agree that the CIO has a strong educational partnership with the CEO and board of directors, and 83% agree that the CIO increasingly needs to rely on trusted advisors to help navigate new technologies, processes, and methodologies.

Both are additional indicators that IT leadership is now inextricably tied to business strategy. In terms of executive status, CIOs increasingly have a direct line report to the CEO, cited by nearly half (49%) of respondents and higher among IT leaders in the financial services (56%) and high-tech (54%) sectors, as well as at SMB organizations (less than 1,000 employees) (57%). CIOs are themselves overseeing some of the newly established C-level roles, such as the Chief Data Officer (53%), Chief Analytics Officer (45%), and the Chief Digital Officer (42%).

CIOs continue to take on responsibilities outside of the IT domain, specifically creating new revenue-generating initiatives. Sixty-eight percent of IT leaders confirmed they currently have some sort of revenue responsibility, up from 65% in the 2022 State of CIO survey and much higher among

IT leaders in the high-tech (88%) and financial services (75%) industries. Forty-four percent of IT leaders manage a team that creates new revenue-generating capabilities, while 24% are part of such a team. In support of making organizations more revenue-driven, CIOs are automating business and IT processes (47%), creating new products and services (40%), and making data more available (34%).

Chasing efficiencies and elevated customer experiences:

Unlike last year, when cybersecurity was the No. 1 business and technology priority, this year it was all about transformation in pursuit of higher efficiencies. Increasing operational efficiency was the top business initiative, cited by 45% of CIO respondents and 33% of LOB respondents, and higher again among manufacturing (54%) and education (54%) companies.

Transforming existing business processes through tactics like automation and integration was the third-ranked objective, cited by 38% of respondents, and improving profitability was the top goal for LOB participants, cited by 34%

Cybersecurity was by no means knocked out of the ring. Increasing cybersecurity protections remained a big deal,

cited by a third of LOB respondents as well as 44% of IT leaders, albeit less than the 49%

Tech initiatives driving IT investments in 2023:	**Business initiatives driving IT investments in 2023:**
1. Security/risk management	1. Increasing operational efficiency
2. Data/business analytics	2. Increasing cybersecurity protections
3. Application/legacy systems modernization	3. Transforming existing business processes
4. Machine learning/ Artificial Intelligence	4. Improving customer experience
5. Customer experience technologies	5. Improving profitability

CIOs getting into the Customer Experience Zone:

2022 State of the CIO research. Security and risk management technologies are still expected to drive the most IT investment in 2023, cited by 38% of IT leader respondents and 30% of LOB. IT leaders also called out data/business analytics (34%), application/ legacy systems modernization (28%), and machine learning/ artificial intelligence (26%) as other target areas for investment. Customer experience remains at the forefront, while employee experience has fallen in Favor as a top priority.

Improving customer experience was the third-ranked CEO mandate, highlighted by 24% of respondents, and a critical business initiative cited by 29% of LOB respondents. Almost half of respondents (49%) said the need to improve customer experience increased in priority as a business initiative due to the current state of the economy.

Organizations are addressing the imperative to enhance customer experience by analyzing customer needs and behaviors (45%), delivering products and services in new ways (42%), and adapting products and services to meet changing demands (40%).

4.4 IT leaders spending time in more places:

Many of this year's technology investments and business initiatives were driven by economic concerns. Fifty-eight percent of IT leaders tied the increased focus on operational efficiency and cyber protections to the current state of the economy, with 54% saying it has amplified attention to transform existing business processes and improve profitability.

Over the next year, CIOs expect to work more closely on technology projects with executive-level administration (including planning, budgeting, and organizing) (53%), along with operations (48%) and finance/ accounting (34%). Surprisingly, the supply chain was not expected to be a critical area.

91% of CIOs expect their organization's overall IT budget to either increase or stay the same over the next 12 months

IT leaders participating in the 2023 State of the CIO research expect to get more involved in areas like security (70%), data analysis (55%), and data privacy/ compliance (55%) while retrenching somewhat on physical security (14%), cloud migration (14%), and supply chain (13%). Their LOB counterparts are anticipating greater CIO involvement in cybersecurity (58%), data privacy/compliance (53%), and product development/innovation (49%). They expect less CIO input in physical security, AI/machine learning, diversity, equity, and inclusion.

While a hot button in corporate and global economic circles, Environmental, Social, and Governance (ESG) is having a marginal impact on the CIO role or IT buying plans.

CIOs are being tasked to adhere to ESG standards and play a role in selecting clean information technology, cited by 64% of IT leaders. However, it is higher in enterprise organizations (70%), EMEA (74%), and APAC (73%) compared to only 51% in North America. Sixty-three percent of IT leader respondents said that ESG standards are an important

63% of tech leaders said ESG standards are an important buying criterion when reviewing tech vendors and partners. Increases to 73% for Enterprise buying criterion when reviewing technology vendors and partners, again is higher at enterprises (73%) and oversees (73% APAC and 70% EMEA).

A smaller number of CIOs said aligning the business to ESG standards has influence over 2023 technology buying plans, specifically 59% of IT leaders and again, higher amongst high-tech IT leader respondents (68%) as well as APAC organizations (71%) and enterprises (66%). LOB respondents saw more potential for corporate ESG goals directly shaping technology purchase plans, cited by 66%.

Budgets remain steady despite economic concerns. While economic uncertainty took a toll on the stock market and companies' financial health, IT budgets came out relatively unscathed. Forty-four percent of LOB respondents and 56% of IT leaders expect IT budgets to increase this year, with 35% and 48%, respectively, expecting things to remain status.

Tech budgets are a part of the overall IT budget for these roles

Chief Analytics Officer 75%

Chief Data Officer 63%

Chief Digital Officer 59%

Number 1 Reason for tech budget increase:

The need for security improvements in comparison, 59% of last year's respondents reported budget increases, which was a significant bump over the 37% reporting a hike in 2021. Companies in the financial services (69%), manufacturing (64%), and government (65%) sectors were more likely to expect increases.

IT leaders indicating a likelihood of budget increases cited the need for security improvements (40%) as the number one motivator, followed by the need to upgrade outdated IT infrastructure (38%) and application modernization (38%). Technology investment for enabling hybrid work was far less of a priority this year, cited by only 22% of respondents and even lower than the 30% last year.

Companies planning IT budget cuts this year (9%) cited economic instability and uncertainty (58%), company finances (49%), and a reduction in employee headcount (38%). IT still retains direct control over a good portion of the IT budget at most companies– on average, around 43.5%. However, IT expects its jurisdiction over IT budgets to tick back upwards to nearly 50% in the next three years.

Titles. For example, 58% of the respondents said the CTO's budget was part of the overall technology expenditures. Half of the respondents said the same for the Chief Digital Officer's budget and 63% of the Chief Data Officer's expenses. Budgets allocated to the Chief Security Officer and Chief Analytics Officer were even more likely to be integrated into overall IT expenditures, at 72% and 75%, respectively.

4.5 The ongoing talent Crunch:

While organizations are still struggling to find seasoned talent in critical skills areas, they aren't prioritizing talent acquisition strategies as much as they have in the past. Improving strategies to acquire and retain talent didn't even rank in the top 10 of the most significant business initiatives driving IT investment. It was cited by only 17% of respondents—slightly higher among education, financial services, and healthcare companies.

Top skills in demand to support digital business initiatives:

1. Technology integration/ implementation

2. IT/cloud architecture

3. Risk/security management

Economy-related challenges are having an impact on prioritizing talent acquisition practices—41% of IT leaders said they were ramping up, and 44% said efforts would remain the same. Only 10% said improving talent acquisition/retention was less of a priority than it had been in the past.

As IT departments look to fill critical skills gaps, they are targeting areas related to modernization and transformation, with technology integration/implementation (42%), IT cloud architecture (40%), and risk/security management (36%) the most in demand. Manufacturing (50%) and financial services (51%) are in most need of integration and implementation prowess, while risk/security management remains a bigger priority for those in the education (54%) and health care (50%) sectors.

Soft skills are another competency area IT organizations are looking to shore up. IT leaders are in search of professionals versed in project management (31%), change management (29%), and strategy building/mapping out a digital business plan (25%). Business relationship management skills are also coveted, cited by a quarter of IT leader respondents.

Not surprisingly, LOB business respondents had a different take on what's required to support digital business initiatives: Customer experience management (31%), project management (29%), and financial/cost management (27%) were high on their wish list. Over the next six to 12 months, IT leaders plan to hire in a few key areas, most notably cybersecurity (39%), application development (30%), and data science.

Anticipating new hires over the next 1 to 2 Yrs. months in:

- Cybersecurity (39%)

- App development (30%)
- Data science/analytics (30%

AI/Machine learning skills are in demand, cited by 26% of respondents, as are candidates with DevOps/DevSecOps and agile experience (24%). The prioritization of these areas over cloud architecture and cloud services/integration competencies indicates that IT leaders are planning and expecting to swing back to digital transformation initiatives once operations and infrastructure modernization are well underway.

IT leaders do anticipate difficulty finding qualified experts, especially in advanced areas such as blockchain (22%), cybersecurity (22%), and data science/analytics (22%). Cutting-edge competencies like AI/ML and robotic process automation are also expected to be difficult to fill when staffing key projects.

Summary:

Despite another year dominated by transformational and functional work, IT leaders are making significant headway on modernizing the IT estate in preparation for the next cycle of digital innovation. In the interim, CIOs are expanding their domains and shoring up relationships, maturing into core leadership roles and cementing their status as strategic partners to the business.

Regional key takeaways: Is your marketing scope region-specific? Explore the key research findings from North America, Europe, and Asia Pacific. Contact us to dive deeper into the regional results.

Budget:

• The #1 reason in NA for a tech budget increase is the need for security improvements • Of those 9% that stated they expect a decrease in their tech budget, the #1 reason is because of company finances/performance

The CIO role:

• 82% of NA CIOs say they are more involved in leading digital transformation initiatives compared to their business counterparts • 84% of NA CIOs agree they are becoming a changemaker, increasingly leading business and technology initiatives • Just over half (51%) of CIOs in NA agreed to the statement that they are IT leaders in the EMEA region (70%)

said that ESG standards are an essential buying criterion when reviewing technology vendors and partners

Business initiatives:

In 2023, the following business initiatives will be most significant in driving IT investments at EMEA organizations: • Increasing cybersecurity protections (47%) • Increasing operational efficiency (42%) • Transforming existing business processes (41%)

Technology initiatives: In 2023, the following technology initiatives will drive the most IT investment at EMEA organizations: • Security/risk management (37%) • Machine learning/AI (31%) • Data/business analytics (30%) • Application/legacy systems modernization (30%) • Cloud infrastructure (30%)

Skills: When asked which skills the IT department is most in need of to support ongoing digital business initiatives, respondents said: • IT/cloud architecture (49%) • Technology integration/ implementation (45%) • Risk/security management (38%)

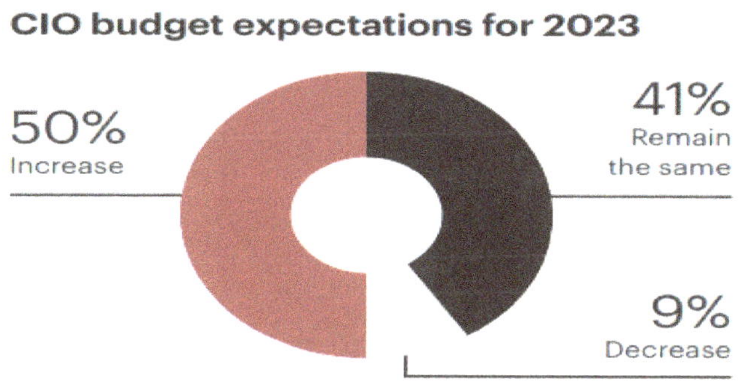

Picture Credit: www.google.com

Europe, Middle East, and Africa **(EMEA)**

CIO budget expectations for 2023

Budget:

• The #1 reason in EMEA for a tech budget increase is modernizing applications. Of that 10% that stated they expect a decrease in their tech budget, the #1 reason is because of economic uncertainty

The CIO role:

- 84% of EMEA CIOs say they are more involved in leading digital transformation initiatives compared to their business counterparts
- 85% of EMEA CIOs agree they are becoming a changemaker, increasingly leading business and technology initiatives
- EMEA CIOs are adhering to Environmental, Social, and Governance (ESG) standards more so than other regions, as 74% of CIOs in this region agreed they CIOs are being tasked to adhere to ESG standards and play a role in selecting clean information technology
- IT leaders in the EMEA region (70%) said that ESG standards are an essential buying criterion when reviewing technology vendors and partners

Business initiatives:

In 2023, the following business initiatives will be most significant in driving IT investments at EMEA organizations: • Increasing cybersecurity protections (47%) • Increasing operational efficiency (42%) • Transforming existing business processes (41%)

Technology initiatives:

In 2023, the following technology initiatives will drive the most IT investment at EMEA organizations: • Security/risk management (37%) • Machine learning/AI (31%) • Data/business analytics (30%) • Application/legacy systems modernization (30%) • Cloud infrastructure (30%)

Skills:

When asked which skills the IT department is most in need of to support ongoing digital business initiatives, respondents said: • IT/cloud architecture (49%) • Technology integration/ implementation (45%) • Risk/security management (38%).

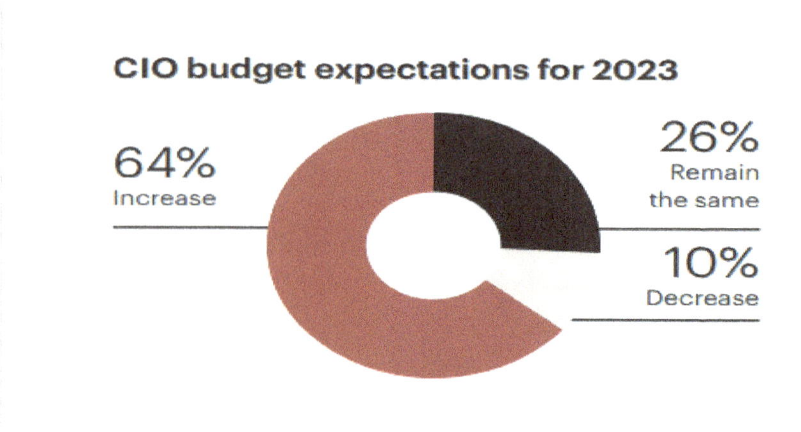

Picture Credit: www.google.com

4.6 IT-Driven Business Innovation

Businesses are being transformed by new technologies, especially those that bring more intelligence and mobility to their operations and products. Some companies are accelerating this transformation by pursuing IT-enabled business innovation as a core strategy throughout their organization, according to a recent Harvard Business Review Analytic Services survey of more than 400 business leaders around the world. Roughly a third of respondents work in these "Innovation Accelerator" companies.

Company Posture

Towards IT-driven Business Innovation

Which of the following best describes your company's posture toward IT-driven business innovation?

Innovation Accelerators

■ In company DNA and consciously pursued strategy throughout the organization

Ad Hoc Innovators

■ Pockets of ad hoc innovation, but not pervasive or replicated across the whole company

Not A Priority

■ Innovation is not a top priority; focus elsewhere

What areas of your business will be most affected by IT-enabled innovation over the next three years?

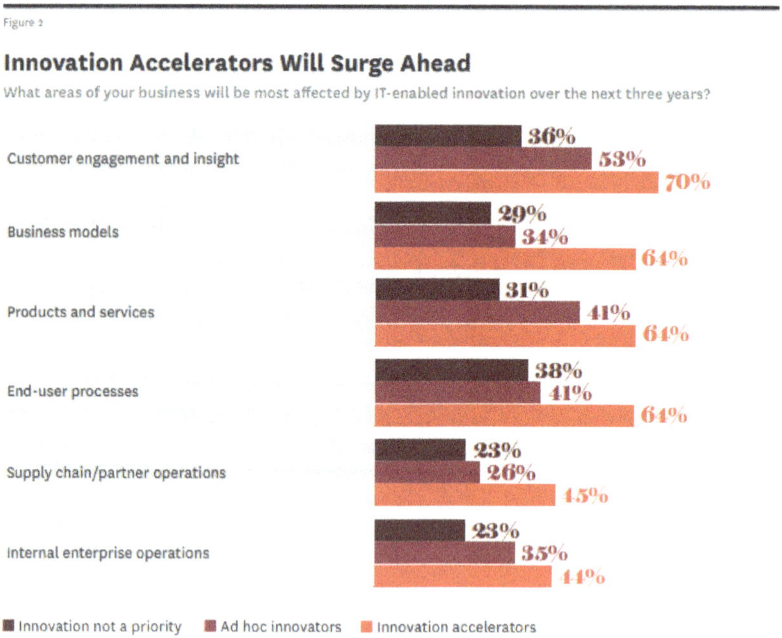

Picture Credit: www.google.com

This translates to several specific projects that respondents expect to engage in over the next three years. Over half said they will automate business processes (67%); execute customer experience strategies (66%); create new applications (60%); and innovate their services (57%) and business models (56%).

Supply chain factors, and showing how that fits into the client's overall global strategy. "We're helping them see the future." Innovation Accelerators are more than twice as likely to invest in the creation of new applications than their non-prioritizing.

Figure 3: They're also more likely to concentrate externally on revenue generated

Figure 3:

Innovation Accelerators Will Invest Which of the following IT-related innovation projects will your business engage in over the next three years?

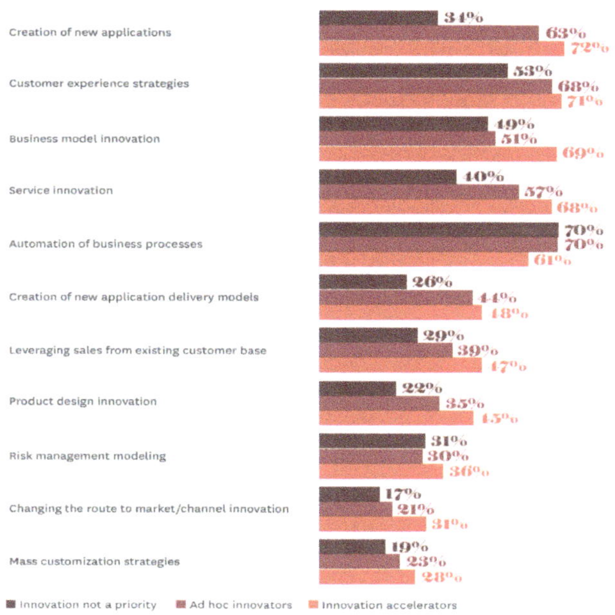

Picture Credit: www.google.com

Which Initiatives Have They Commercialized?

What types of IT initiatives has your company commercialized?

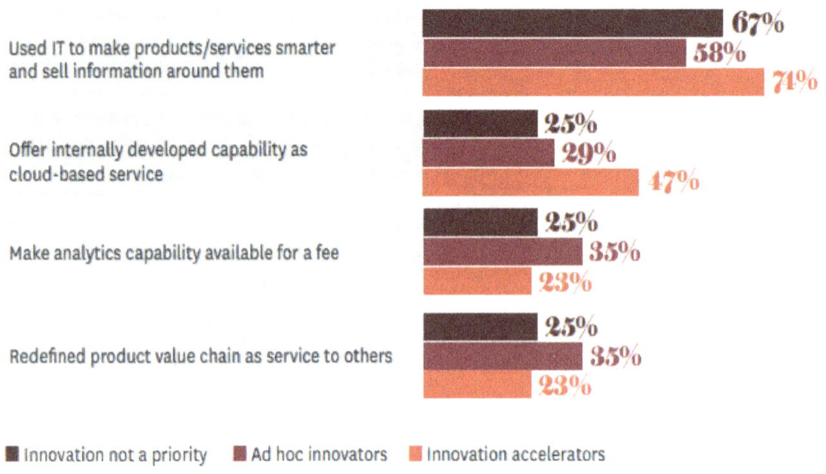

Picture Credit: www.google.com

Opportunities with new customer experience strategies (71%), business model innovation (69%), and service innovation (68%).

By contrast, companies for which innovation is not a priority will focus more internally on the automation of business processes (70%).

Given the focus on customer insight and engagement, it's no surprise that business intelligence/analytics and mobile technologies and apps lead the list of technologies that will drive business innovation over the next three years, at 66% and 53%, respectively.

Process automation, collaboration tools, cloud computing, and social media follow these. Echoing the previous finding, while 56% of Low Prioritizes cited process automation, only 29% of Accelerators did. This likely reflects that these companies have already completed this work and have moved on to other things.

Innovation Accelerators are increasing the return on their technology investments by commercializing some of their internal IT; 40% of them are doing so, compared to only 25% of Ad Hoc innovators and 16% of Low Prioritises. The leading area of opportunity is using IT to make products smarter and to sell the insight such innovative products generate. Figure 4 For example, a diversified industrial manufacturer uses data gleaned through their increasingly tech-enabled equipment on their customers' factory floors to help them improve their operations. Ultimately, they will turn their data analytics services into revenue streams.

Given the top-line potential of such initiatives, investing in and forging an organization-wide commitment to IT-driven business innovation makes sense. Accelerators are more than twice as likely as others to rate their organization's IT innovation better than that of others in their industry (61% vs. 30% for ad hoc innovators and 16% for low priorities), presenting a clear opportunity for competitive advantage. **figure 5**

The Six Characteristics of Innovation Accelerators

Organizations that have made this commitment share some common characteristics.

INNOVATION LEADERSHIP STARTS AT THE TOP

As information technology permeates more top-line activities, the leadership of technology-driven business innovation is shifting. CIOs led this type of innovation—either alone or together with a business partner—in 41% of organizations today. Figure 6 - That figure drops to 34% in Accelerator companies. CEO leadership, on the other hand, increases from 16% to 23%, and other C-level executives combined.

Strength of IT Innovation vs. Industry Peers

How do you think IT innovation in your organization as a whole compare to other businesses in your industry?

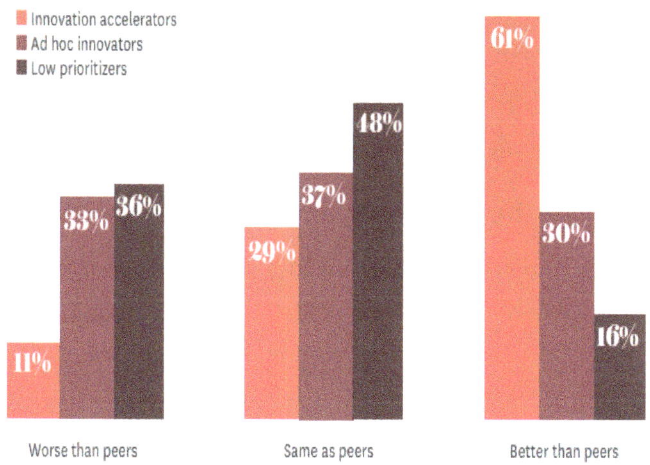

Picture Credit: www.google.com

Accelerators, however, are much more likely to take a structured approach (79%). The global real estate company, for instance, has a formal process for employees to submit ideas, with a tiered system of rewards and recognitions based on the nature of the innovation.

A cross-functional team vets the ideas, with marketing considering its potential from the customer perspective, PR evaluating its "story" potential, IT assessing how it will work with existing systems, etc. Innovation is also part of all employee performance conversations.

While having a structured approach is critical to increasing the flow and uptake of ideas, too much process can bog things down. Executives interviewed for this report talked about the need for speed. "We don't have two or three years to fix this," said the CIO for a regional grocery chain that finds itself competing now with the likes of Walmart and Amazon.

His company uses an enterprise social networking/ collaboration tool to move ideas quickly from the edge (store managers, associates, and even customers) to the organization's centre. All executives receive a daily digest of posts culled from the tool; the contents are discussed at executive staff meetings.

Cross-training and departmental rotations can help speed innovation efforts by giving people a shared understanding of the business, according to several executives interviewed for this report.

The CIO at the large state government agency had previously worked in different lines of business and had run one of them. She used her common understanding to engage her business partners in brainstorming sessions around their biggest pain points and desires. Together, they conceived and gained approval for the massive innovation project with the 7:1 return.

Who Is Responsible for Innovation?

Who's primarily responsible for leading a) technology-driven business innovation and b) other innovation from a strategic or content perspective?

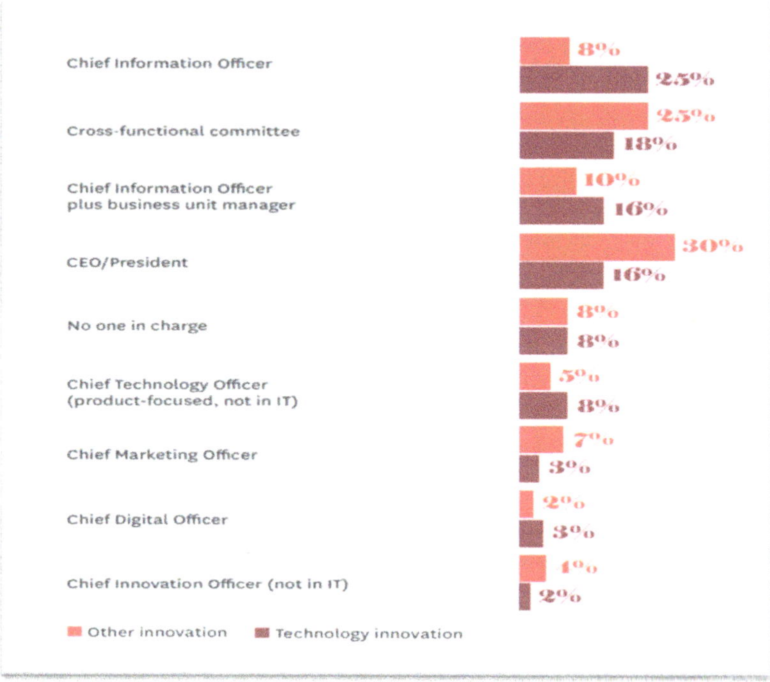

Picture Credit: www.google.com

Outdated legacy technology can act as a drag on innovation efforts, and many organizations are trying to modernize as quickly as they can. “We’re aggressive because we’re on catch-up,” said the CTO of a luxury goods company. “The way we attack that is with agile methodology—that’s a best practice within the group.” The company is working toward having a single platform across all the brands, both for their back office and how they engage with customers, but that will take time.

Rather than wait for the entire project to be completed and rolled out in a “big bang,” he uses what he calls a “little and often” methodology. “We need to be moving forward every day,” he explained. “If you’re doing agile, you create a continuous readiness for change.” He’s careful to strike a balance, however. “We don’t want to overload the organization; you must allow it to settle.”

Experienced leaders have learned that a good marketing campaign can facilitate IT-driven change. “You have to have a sales and marketing mentality,” said the CIO at an East Coast university. “All our services have to be desired—that’s how you get a fast uptake.” If you can generate buzz around the roll-out of a system, then "the next project will be easier, faster, better."

To induce that desire, however, requires understanding how the business works—what people are trying to do and where their frustrations lie.

NEW PERSPECTIVES

Innovation Accelerators know the value of cross-functional collaboration; almost half (48%) say that IT and the business typically engage together to identify innovation opportunities.

Ad hoc innovators and low priorities were both more likely to take a business-led approach, with the IT Department in a supporting role, implementing new technology requirements that it receives from the business but not participating up front.

A large consumer goods company whose products have been disrupted by a combination of government regulations and new competition has changed its culture dramatically in this regard. "There's great recognition and inclusion across different functions for innovation and work processes," said the director of sales and marketing technology.

It's becoming the norm to reach beyond a particular group for help solving problems. Staff meetings are open to people from other functions, and there's a new emphasis on "going two levels down" to expose executives to the people doing the work to identify opportunities for simplification.

Accelerators are much more likely to have a cross-functional innovation board and to take an open approach to innovation through crowd-sourcing and encouraging end-user ideas.

Figure 7 "We don't prejudge who might be able to solve the problem," said a department leader at a large government agency that uses both internal and external crowd-sourcing to tackle technical challenges. The university CIO encourages everyone to weigh in; one night, when he was working late, he got a valuable suggestion to improve the new company intranet from a member of the facilities team. Such instances are publicized and celebrated to encourage more engagement. Major transformations require bringing in people with a different experience base. The luxury goods company hired from the online trading world to help it transition to e-commerce because it was so different from its traditional retail environment.

IT-driven Business Innovation Tactics: A Close-up

Which of the following approaches to IT-driven business innovation does your company employ, if any?

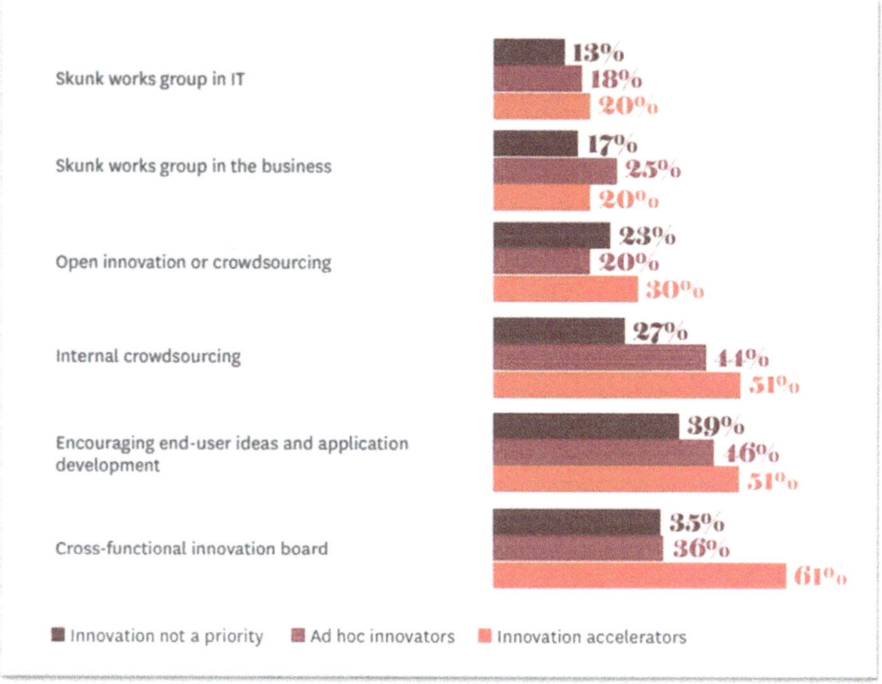

Picture Credit: www.google.com

4.7 CIOS ARE BUSINESS STRATEGISTS

CIOs have a mandate to innovate in this changing environment. However, the daily concerns of running IT and inadequate resources often hold them back. While 57% of respondents say the CIO should drive innovation and strategy, only 12% say their CIO does that. figure 8

Respondents perceive their CIOs as spending most of their time on functional activities, alignment, and change. Figure 9 Almost half say their CIO focuses on cost control/expense management and managing IT crises; few say these activities add value to the business. Conversely, almost half say the CIO should spend time on driving business innovation, but only 16% say they do. Forty percent say the CIO should identify opportunities for competitive differentiation; only 13% say they do.

To be fair, some of this may be perception. In a similar study conducted by CIO magazine, respondents— all of whom were themselves CIOs—indicated they spend slightly more time on Business Strategist activities than was reported in this study, significantly more time on Transformational activities, and significantly less time on Functional tasks, generally speaking.

But things are looking brighter at Accelerator companies, where CIOs are significantly more likely to spend time on activities that are strategic to the business. These include developing and refining business strategy (26% at Accelerators compared to 13% at Ad Hoc and 14% at Low prioritizes);

driving business innovation (30% v 10% and 5%); and identifying opportunities for competitive differentiation (26% v 7% and 9%). And CIOs are increasingly called upon to go on sales calls to explain a new tech-enabled value proposition to prospects and customers.

Accelerator CIOs focus on the strategic priorities and metrics that matter. For a competency-based online university, that means increasing graduation rates to equate not just to other online universities but to traditional higher ed. We looked at what levers we can pull to increase graduation rates by 10 percent.

CIOs' Actual vs. Ideal Role

Which of the following best represents the current role of your organization's CIO?

Which of the following CIO roles would enable the most valuable and effective technology-driven business innovation in your organization in the future?

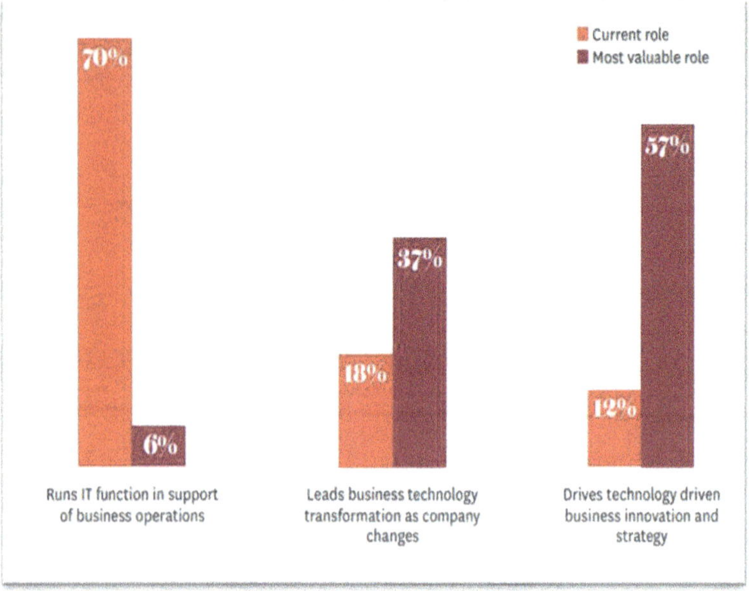

Picture Credit: www.google.com

How the CIO Spends His/her Time

Which of the following activities best characterize how your current CIO spends his or her time?

Which of the following activities should that person spend time on to add the most value to the business?

		What Business Leaders Say[1]		What CIOs Say[1]	
		TODAY	IDEAL	TODAY	3 YEARS
BIZ-STRATEGIST	Developing and refining business strategy	17%	32%	20%	32%
	Studying market trends/customer needs to identify commercial opportunities	12%	26%	8%	25%
	Driving business innovation	16%	46%	18%	41%
	Identifying opportunities for competitive differentiation	13%	40%	15%	43%
	Developing new go-to-market strategies and technologies	12%	32%	13%	23%
TRANSFORMATIONAL	Redesigning business processes	15%	28%	17%	23%
	Aligning IT initiatives with business goals	36%	44%	45%	35%
	Cultivating the IT/business partnership	26%	36%	40%	42%
	Leading change efforts	22%	33%	38%	26%
	Implementing new systems and architecture	40%	21%	47%	27%
FUNCTIONAL	Managing IT crises	45%	8%	22%	6%
	Negotiating with IT vendors	38%	7%	29%	13%
	Improving IT operations/systems performance	41%	27%	48%	16%
	Security management	41%	16%	29%	13%
	Cost control/expense management	49%	16%	35%	16%

Picture Credit: www.google.com

This framework is from the CIO Executive Council Future State CIO model

1. Results from the current survey

2. Data from the Market Pulse survey conducted by CIO magazine for Red Hat in which respondents answered for their position points over the next 5 years," said the CIO. "If you consider us an e-commerce company, we have a customer retention problem. So we're working on customer intimacy, segmentation, and filling the needs of those customer profiles." It supports other aspects of the business by standardizing and buying packages wherever possible.

IT SUPPORTS NEW BUSINESS OPPORTUNITIES

Today's IT departments are not well positioned to support the innovation agenda, according to survey respondents. When asked how they would characterize their company's current IT organization, most said they viewed them as a cost centre (29%) or service provider (33%).

Only 20% see them as a trusted partner, and few view them as a peer or business game changer (16% combined). Figure 10 Once again, Accelerators portray a different picture, with 30%—almost twice as many—viewing their IT departments as a peer or game changer, and only 13% regarding them as a cost centre (compared to Low Prioritizes' 53%).

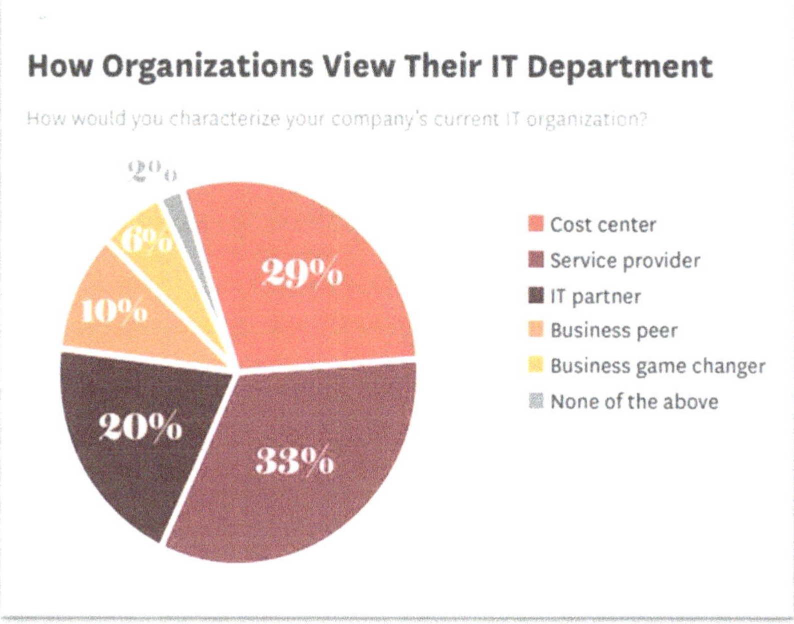

Picture Credit: www.google.com

Innovation Accelerators have IT departments that are highly capable of supporting new business ideas and opportunities. Figure 11 They are much more likely to have access to the right technology, knowledge of the business, and the right technical skills and to be more receptive to new ideas. They are also more than twice as likely to have the right IT talent to drive their business innovation agenda, with 62% saying they do, compared to 31% of Ad Hoc Innovators and 27% of Low Priorities.

Accelerators' IT departments are far more likely to have a good understanding of the business, communicate effectively with senior business leaders, and possess the skills to ensure future company success. Figure 12 They proactively identify new technologies to fuel innovation and invest in technology that supports engagement with their senior business leaders. It is clear: Companies that have prioritized innovation have strong IT departments that actively and productively contribute to the corporate innovation agenda.

INVEST IN AND REWARD INNOVATION

Sometimes, having the right skills, mindset, and ability is not enough; investment in innovation is important too. "Our CIO has that ability," said the Controller at a global asset management company. "The challenge is we haven't had the resources to act on that. We've been in keep-the-lights on mode," with the technology budget limited to maintaining existing systems and doing required upgrades. This year, he said, additional resources are being freed up to do new things.

A good place to put such investment is in an emerging technologies group; Innovation Accelerators are twice as likely as Ad Hoc Innovators or Low Priorities to fund such groups (63% vs. 30% and 32%). However, investing in innovation doesn't have to mean breaking the bank. Sometimes, it means being creative on a very lean budget indeed. The consumer goods company has an IT budget of less than 1.5% of revenue.

"It's difficult to free up headcount and dollars to invest in experimental projects when you're scrambling just to maintain operations," said the director of sales and marketing technology. Their solution has been to create "innovation challenges" in which a cross-functional team works together for four or five days to solve a specific business problem.

Sometimes, they include customers. As ideas show promise, they earn more investment. So far, three of the nine challenges they've run have yielded commercial products. A significant side benefit is that "it's taught people to work differently," and that's carried over into their everyday lives.

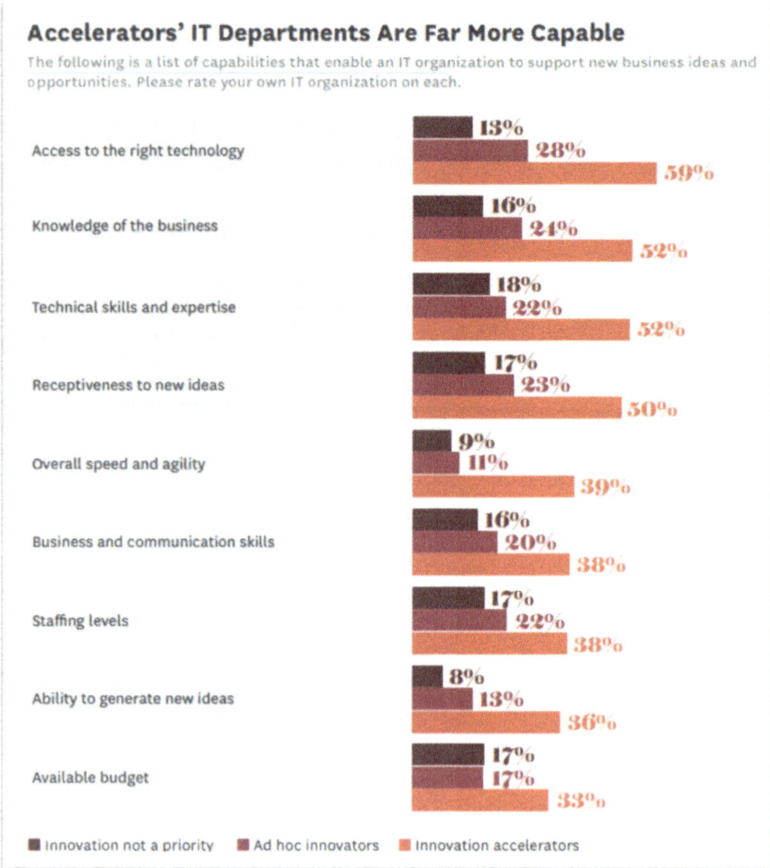

Picture Credit: www.google.com

A global software company brings its IT team together a couple of times a year for an innovation contest. Senior executives present their biggest problems, and people compete to come up with solutions.

The winners get money to go and implement their solution. A government agency engages its employees through internal crowd-sourcing for ideation problems. It goes outside for specific modelling problems, using such partners as Innovative, a global crowd-sourcing platform, to tap into the broader scientific community.

"We've moved from the vertically organized institutions of the past to use significant outside resources to best advantage," said a department leader. "The main challenge is integrating this innovation process into our existing project flow." Accelerators are also more likely to consult with futurists to visit technology labs and to reward innovation (56% of Innovation Accelerators are rewarded for innovation versus only 35% of Ad Hoc Innovators and 19% of Low Prioritizes). While rewards can be financial, often recognition and the ability to work on interesting projects have a greater impact.

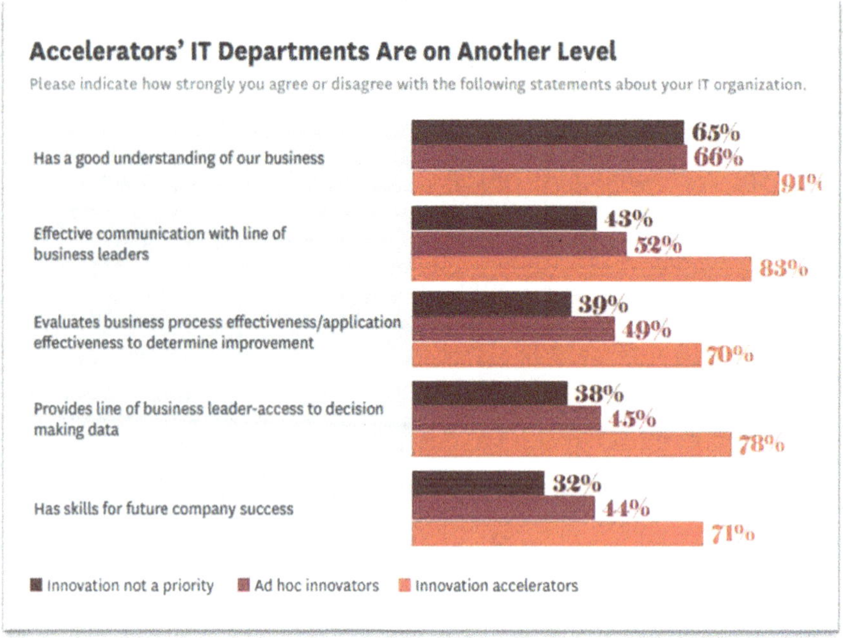

Picture Credit: www.google.com

Conclusion

Rapid developments in information technology—especially analytics and mobile technologies - are having a dramatic impact on all aspects of business. This research suggests that organizations that make a strong commitment to IT-driven business innovation will accelerate their transformation in such key areas as how they engage with and understand their customers, new business models, the development of new products and services, how employees do their work, and more.

These Innovation Accelerators are significantly ahead of their competitors when it comes to IT innovation–including the extent to which they have successfully commercialized internal IT initiatives. The research also reveals six key characteristics these Accelerator companies share that can help provide a roadmap for others seeking to transform their businesses. It begins with a commitment from the CEO that is shared by the company's cross-functional leadership. It includes taking a structured approach to ensure innovation occurs throughout the organization without bogging it down.

Innovation Accelerators are inclusive, valuing the perspectives, knowledge, and ideas of diverse people and groups, both inside and outside the company. They have strong CIOs who focus on business strategy and innovation and identify opportunities for competitive differentiation. They have IT departments that support new business ideas and opportunities with access to the right technology, knowledge of the business, and the right technical skills. And they invest in and reward innovation. CIOs have a mandate to innovate.

The ones who accelerate won't wait for permission but will lead their organizations into what will likely be a very different, technology-driven future. They will be a key part of the CEO's growth team, designing the open, agile, and customer-engaged organization that will create new value—and competitive advantage.

5. Understanding the CIO's Role in Enhancing Customer Experience (CX)

Focusing on the customer makes a company more resilient. "The most important thing is to obsessively focus on the customer. It's our job every day to make every important aspect of the customer experience a little bit better."

-Jeff Bezos

5.1 Overview

Fail Fast Approach to Achieve Your Customer Experience (CX)

My recent article, which was published in the Singapore Magazine Interview with Genesys, is all about linking the Fail Fast concept to Customer Experience. The Fail Fast Approach is optimizing the speed of execution for any product or service you are planning to launch, trying to build a successful product by taking continuous incremental feedback and developing, testing, and implementing once again. Reiterate the same process till your product is a success and starts creating value.

However, success doesn't happen overnight. Building a successful product requires continuous improvement based on customer feedback.

So, what is the right way to implement this approach for any product, service, or start-up business you are planning?

1. **Top-line matrix**
2. **Technology, innovation, and digital transformation**
3. **Customer experience**

You need to identify the **Top Line Matrix** required for the pre-launch and post-launch of your product. In today's world, the business landscape is changing rapidly. There is a need to consider multiple factors that affect the business - launching a start-up, product, or service with new technology, customer mindset, demographic changes, a new competitor in the market having a similar product, political changes bringing new dimensions - and so on.

Even if you launch the product successfully and gather a massive response in the market, you must evaluate how many customers are using your product and renewing their licenses. Your product should be unique, and you need to identify who is your actual customer, whether this product is for B2B customers or B2C customers. Who is your competitor? How is your product beneficial for customers compared to competitor products? You need to have a user-specific UI/UX journey as a customer group and a similar mindset.

For example, if the customer is in the 18-40 age group or 60-80 age group, the user journey will be different. There are retail customers and HNI customers, and your product has to be designed accordingly to provide the best customer experience to the set of customers you are targeting.

"Keep in mind that people buy experiences and not only the product." You will retain your customers only when you provide a better customer experience with the help of the latest technology and digital transformation. So, connect with your customers, get continuous feedback, and embed that incrementally and iteratively.

The second parameter is the customer touch point. In today's world, connecting with your customers and keeping them engaged with unique features and ideas is paramount. There are multiple ways you can keep in touch with your customers - through a website, WhatsApp, chatbot, social media like LinkedIn, Facebook, and Twitter, and one-to-one interactive sessions, which will help to retain your existing customers.

I would like to add one more parameter - your organization's employees need to be trained to deliver a better customer experience. The organization's culture should support continuous improvement in customer experience (CX) with the help of the Fail Fast Approach.

I will share my personal experience when I started to change our employee's mindset towards customer experience (CX). 1st thing we did with the help of the branding team was fix various customer experience pictures on the wall and entry where employees work.

The other thing we had created was a specific award category for customer experience (CX) with award cash vouchers and certificates.

Finally, we provided various pieces of training and brought awareness among employees "why customer experience is the key to success'." It is not easy to change culture and people's mindsets; it is a continuous journey. There are multiple steps we need to take to change our culture and employee mindset, which is very important.

What happens when you don't implement the Fail Fast Approach?

If you are unable to deliver a product or service with a Fail Fast Approach, eventually, your product or service will not meet customer expectations, and you will lose business. Lack of technology, innovation, and ideation is the reason why most companies are unable to strike a chord with their end customers.

For example, **Kodak**, a technology company that dominated the photographic film market during the 20th century, was not able to meet customer expectations due to a lack of digital transformation.

Mobile companies like Nokia and Motorola were the global leaders of their time, but they failed to meet customer expectations due to a lack of technological innovation.

In 2005, **Yahoo** was one of the leading players in the online advertising market. But it undervalued the importance of Search.

BlackBerry, a line of smartphones and tablets, was successful in 1998. They changed the game in the mobile industry by offering a device with an arched keyboard. But eventually, they lost the market position because they failed to innovate and keep up with the competition.

Google Glass, the product, was one of the first large-scale attempts at capitalizing on artificial reality. But when the product was launched in 2015, its high price and privacy concerns, combined with a general lack of awareness of consumer needs, never saw the product go mainstream.

Here are companies who implemented a Fail Fast Approach, met customer expectations, and redeveloped their business model only to succeed.

Netflix is an example of a company disrupting an entire industry with amazing customer experience.

Ikea's novel idea of self-assembling furniture, a cleverly planned layout, and a digitized supply chain helped them solve the worst furniture challenges and deliver an excellent customer experience.

Uber, Amazon, and Apple were able to deliver the best customer experience with the help of the latest technology and continuously innovate with the Fail Fast approach, which alternately took their business to the next level and retained customers.

The Key takeaway is If you do not Fail Fast, you will not be able to succeed and deliver the best customer experience product. The best product is not an overnight job; it is a continuous effort to build the best product, service, or platform with the help of new technology, innovation, and digital transformation. This applies to organizations or individuals looking to launch a new start-up business, product, or service.

In today's digital age, it's crucial to me, as the head of IT or CIO, that I understand what that customer sentiment is and how we can go about improving it.

Only CIOs can see how technology can help with each step, and - in collaboration with the CX team - they can map each touchpoint. This customer journey overview is critical to resolving all potential bottlenecks and other issues. CIOs are integral to CX because they can utilize data analytics, artificial intelligence (AI), and personalization tools to understand customer needs better and expand the reach of a business to meet your customers on their terms.

CIO, to follow in a CEO's footsteps, will need to take ownership of information and better align with business needs and Customer Experience (CX). One of the most significant changes in the role of CIOs has been the shift from a focus on customer service to **customer-centricity**.

They have a holistic view of where the data is stored and access to the tools and systems used by other business functions. They are in the perfect position to integrate these disparate systems and put themselves in the customers' shoes. It's been a maniacal focus of mine over the last four years, improving CX.

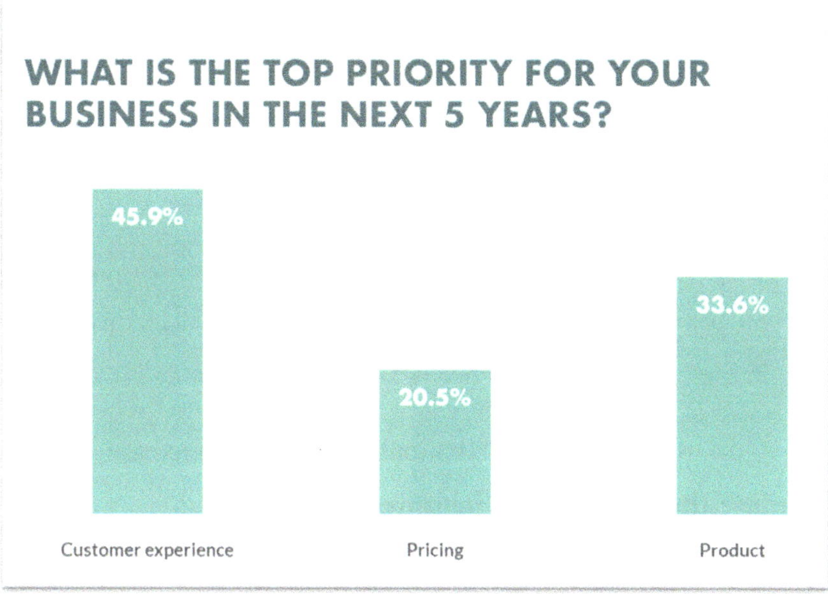

Picture Credit: www.google.com

"Harvard Business Review (HBR) research shows that nearly ***9 out of 10*** *customers say they've left a company, switching due to poor Customer Experience (CX)".* Customer experience is a key focus area for the

majority of executives across a broad of industries, regions, and company sizes.

Are you Ready to increase your investment and improve your customers ` experience?

Put simply:

Companies that successfully implement a customer experience strategy achieve higher customer satisfaction rates, reduced customer churn, and increased revenues.

Sounds like a win-win, right?

Surprisingly, **less than half** of all organizations will be investing in the customer experience next year.

Our research found that **only 44% will increase their investment in their CX initiatives.**

Picture Credit: www.google.com

According to a global CX study by Oracle, **74% of senior executives** believe that customer experience impacts the willingness of a customer to be a loyal advocate. If you want your customers to stay loyal, you have to invest in their experience.

You must focus on the experience you deliver to your customers.

For example, here's a few statistics that caught our eye:

- Customer experience is set to be **the number one brand differentiator in recent years**

- **1 in 3 customers** will leave a brand they love after just one bad experience,
- Customers are willing **to pay a price premium of up to 13%** (and as high as 18%) for luxury and indulgence services simply by receiving a great customer experience,
- **49% of buyers** have made impulse purchases after receiving a more personalized customer experience.
- Customers that rate companies with a high customer experience score (i.e., 10/10) **spend 140% more** and **remain loyal for up to 6 years**.

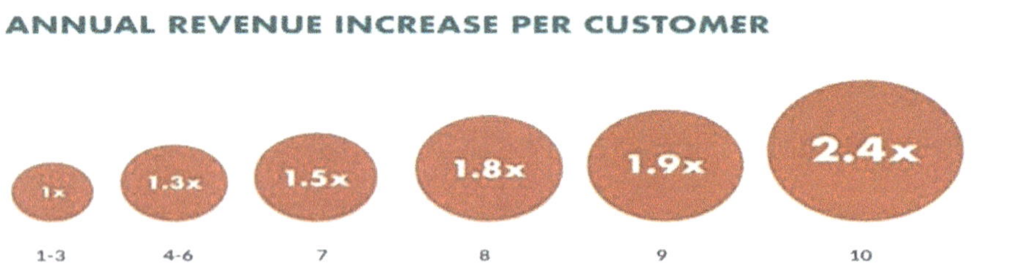

Picture Credit: www.google.com

The challenge here is that even though it's a high priority, most companies are failing to deliver a good customer experience.

So how many brands are truly delivering an excellent customer experience?

Surprisingly, not too many.

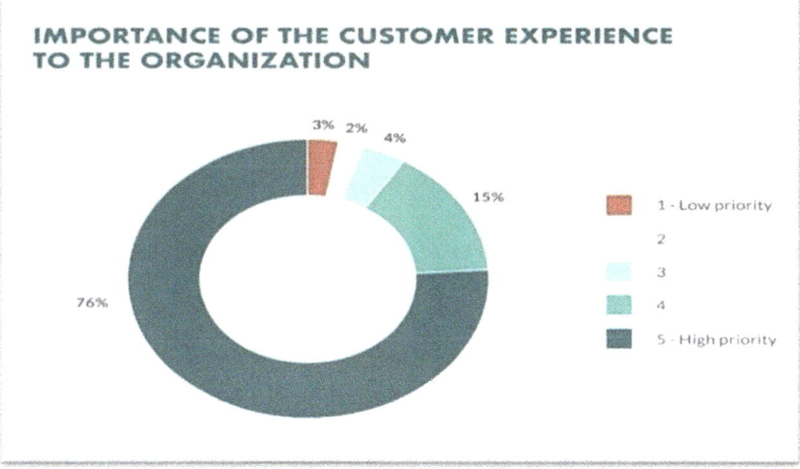

Picture Credit: www.google.com

5.2 Keeping your customers happy is key to the success of your business:

This is why customer experience (CX) has been such a hot topic across sectors, even before the pandemic. Post-pandemic, CIOs and tech professionals delivering digital transformation plans will need to continue focusing on CX as a core business priority to ensure the adoption of revolutionary new technologies amongst the customer base.

Picture Credit: www.google.com

"I've learned that people will forget what you said, people will forget what you did, but people will never forget how you made them feel." "If you are not taking care of your customers, your competitor will." "Building a good customer experience does not happen by accident. It happens by design."

A **positive customer experience** is the most effective way to increase customer satisfaction and engagement. Numerous studies support that improving customer experience can significantly impact a brand's profitability, client retention, and growth.

On the flip side, **poor customer experiences create unhappy customers**. And *did you know that unhappy customers are expensive?*

Customers left with a bad taste after interacting with your company or brand are more likely not to buy from you, now or in the future. Moreover, they can cause you reputational damage and loss of valuable referrals if they decide to share their experience with friends or broadcast it on social media. According to Forbes, dissatisfied customers translate into billions in lost revenue every year for brands worldwide. In financial terms, poor **customer experience (CX)** can impact your organization's bottom line.

According to Temkin, the "Godfather of Customer Experience," the key components of customer experience are the following three:

Success: Was the customer's interaction successful? Were they able to accomplish their initial goals and fulfil their needs when interacting with your business?

Effort: Did the company make it easy for the customer to interact with them, and how much effort did the customer have to put forth?

Emotion: How did the customer feel during and after the interaction? Were they upset or delighted after their experience with your company or brand?

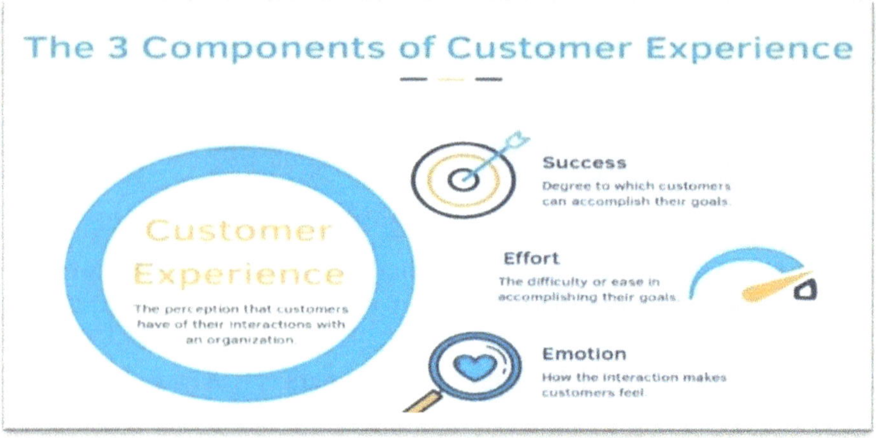

Picture Credits : www.google.com

Of all three components, *Emotion* has the strongest impact on customers' overall impression of a company, their loyalty, and their likeness to purchase more, suggests *Temkin.*

5.3 Why does Customer Experience Matter?

Customer experience can make or break your business.

81% of companies view customer experience as a competitive differentiator.

84% of companies that work to improve their customer experience report increased revenue.

Brands with superior customer experience bring in 5.7 times more revenue than competitors that lag in customer experience.

A **positive customer experience** can be the catalyst for a happy and loyal customer base, who are more likely to:

- **Spend More Money**

Harvard Business Review research identified a direct link between customer experience and annual revenue. Specifically, they found that customers with the best brand experience spent 140% more than those with a bad or less positive experience. Therefore, a satisfying brand experience can **boost sales conversions** and result in **higher customer lifetime value (CLV)**.

- **Come Back for More**

A superior experience **boosts customers' satisfaction** and encourages them to buy from your company multiple times. According to *Qualtrics,* leading companies in CX have customers who are 7x more likely to purchase more from them and 8x more likely to try additional products and services they sell. Hence, creating a good experience gives your business **longevity** and ensures that your customers will keep doing business with you in the future.

- **Stick with You for Life**

Customers with a history of positive experiences with your products or services are more likely to become emotionally attached to your brand. Moreover, they will want to be associated with your business for a lifetime and always choose you over your competitors. In numbers, a satisfied customer has a lifetime value of up to 10 times more than a one-time customer. Simply put, **happy customers stay loyal**.

- **Become your Brand's Ambassadors**

The best marketing a business can ask for is a customer who will promote its products and services through word-of-mouth, recommend them to friends and family members, and advocate for them on social media. Happy customers can do that for you by sharing experiences with the world that will generate a positive buzz around your brand.

On the other hand, **negative customer experiences** create unsatisfied and bitter clients. Some of the consequences of having an unhappy customer base include:

- **Tarnished Name and Reputation**

The impact of unhappy customers extends well beyond your customer bubble. Dissatisfied customers tell twice as many people (between 9-15 people on average) about their negative experiences as happy customers do about their positive experiences. And they hardly ever tell you directly what went wrong or allow you to fix it. Instead, they complain to their social networks (friends, family, colleagues, etc.), **share their bad experiences with your brand** on social media, and leave bad reviews online to prevent others from doing business with you.

- **Loss of Customers**

Over 80% of customers stop doing business with a company after one bad customer experience. Poor CX disseminates a sentiment of neglect to customers, and when they don't feel valued or respected, they take their business elsewhere. But it's not only **current customers** that may be lost due to negative customer experiences. **Potential customers** may be discouraged from using a new product or service linked to a company with a bad reputation. Moreover, almost half of today's consumers won't consider interacting with a company or brand with mostly bad reviews and less than a four-star rating.

- **Loss of Profits**

Poor CX is often the number one reason behind reduced customer interaction with a business. And fewer customers mean lower profits. Unhappy customers won't just stop doing business with you; they will turn to your competitors and encourage others to do the same. Less profit also means a limited budget to improve your customer experience strategy, hence, fewer chances of attracting future customers. To sum up, dissatisfied customers can drain your company's revenue and stability - and that's not an overstatement.

- **Loss of Potential Partners and Employees**

A reputation for bad customer experiences can be enough to **discourage potential employees and other businesses** from doing business with your company. After all, poor CX reflects a lack of care, and potential candidates and other partners will assume that if customers are not treated with sufficient respect and care, they won't be either.

- **Low Retention Rate**

Dealing with customers daily is already challenging. But being subject to anger from dissatisfied customers is a heavy-duty not many are willing to undertake. Especially with sufficient strategies in place to resolve complaints, employees are likely to feel satisfied with their jobs. Eventually, **unhappy employees**, like customers, will leave your company and seek employment elsewhere - probably in companies that provide **effective customer service structures**.

- **Increased Expenses**

Companies with damaged reputations may see their spending increase in their attempt to restore some of the bruises, from expensive rebranding campaigns to new CX and marketing strategies. Moreover, **the real cost of losing a customer** due to poor customer experience is higher than you might think. There is not only the apparent economic loss a customer represents but also the hidden costs of replacing them. Studies have shown that acquiring a new client is 5x more expensive than keeping an existing customer.

The impacts of a positive vs negative customer experience at a glance:

Picture Credit: www.google.com

5.4 What is the Definition of a Good Customer Experience?

Gartner defines customer experience as *"Customer's perceptions and related feelings caused by the one-off and cumulative effect of interactions with a supplier's employees, systems, channels or products."*

A good customer experience makes it easy and pleasant for a customer to do business with you. It also helps customers accomplish their goals when interacting with your company or using your products and services. But most importantly, **great CX makes your customers feel** good during and after their journey with your brand.

These are some of the **factors that constitute an exquisite customer experience**:

- **Personalized Interactions:**

A personalized approach is a must in enhancing customer satisfaction. According to Microsoft, 1/3 of people find the absence of a real person to solve their issues highly frustrating, leaving them with bad CX.

- **Convenience:**

An environment that is easy to access and convenient to comprehend and use can greatly influence customer experience.

- **Transparency:**

Being honest and authentic to your customers also means setting realistic expectations about your brand, products, or services. This way, you can only exceed their expectations and never fail them.

- **Responsiveness:**

Quick response time and always-available customer support reassure customers that you take them seriously and that their opinions, feedback, or complaints are of great value to your company.

- **User-Friendly Technology:**

Businesses that use advanced technologies can delve deeper into their customers' needs and expectations and – consequently – find innovative solutions to enhance the customer experience.

- **Flawless Digital Interactions:**

From reaching your customers through their preferred channel to providing multi-lingual customer support, an easy-to-navigate and user-friendly website, simplified check-out options, multiple payment methods, and everything in between can help you create a pleasant CX.

More importantly, all these factors must work together to create a seamless, consistent, and enhanced experience at every touchpoint of the customer's journey.

5 Examples of Good Customer Experience

To further showcase why a good customer experience is vital for any business, we selected some of the best strategies implemented by industry giants. Let's dive into five notable CX examples and discover how famous brands are ensuring their audiences' loyalty and engagement:

Example #1: Amazon's Delivery Stations

Even with its current success, ***Amazon*** is constantly working to sharpen its shipping standards. Living up to its promise of fast delivery and minimal effort, the company is opening more than a thousand parcel-delivery stations in suburban U.S. locations to support local operations. This further narrows the gap between its fulfilment centres and shipping points and allows the online retail giant to enhance its unique selling point: **same-day delivery**. Amazon knows what its clients want and is not afraid to invest time and money.

Example #2: Apple's Community Hubs

Apple doesn't want to sell innovative products and services – it is committed to turning itself into an "experience ."The company's emerging store layouts are just a part of Apple's effort to become a **central community hub** that prompts face-to-face interactions and allows connections with customers on a personal level. Every store is a living and vibrant part of the community, where Apple experts meet with customers directly, offering a human face to the multi-trillion-dollar company.

Example #3: Burberry's AR Tool

In partnership with Google, ***Burberry*** has developed an Augmented Reality (AR) tool that takes advantage of Google's well-known data and geolocation advantages. The brand's online shoppers can now measure an outfit's size in real-time compared to other items or outfits in their immediate surroundings. The AR tool enhances the **personalization of luxury retail**, allowing customers to try on Burberry's product line from the privacy of their homes.

Example #4: Tesla's Outstanding Customer Service

Tesla's electric vehicles have been leading the way in revolutionizing the automotive industry. But, to make it happen, the company has had to take customer service to the next level. Knowing that what customers cherish the most is convenience, *Tesla* is offering its services directly to their homes. Whether it's a flat tire or an electrical gripe, Tesla's clients know that a team will arrive at their door to fix the issue within the day.

Example #5: Netflix's Customer-Focused Strategy

Netflix is primarily a data-driven company that uses complex internal algorithms to offer each Netflix user a **personalized and unique customer experience**. As you might already know, when logged in, no two people see the same streaming recommendations on their Netflix profile. You might need to know that all the thumbnails you see are also completely personalized to you as a viewer based on what you have watched, clicked, and searched.

5.5 Top 10 Customer Experience (CX) Trends for 2023 & 2024

Your ultimate goal as a business should be to make your audience happy and convert them into loyal customers who can help you boost revenue. Here are **seven tips to improve your customer experience**:

1. Map your Customers' Journey

Before you start investing all your time and resources into a strategy you think might improve your customer experience, it's probably best to have an action plan in place. In most cases, creating a **customer journey map** is a great place to start.

A customer journey map illustrates every step your customers take when interacting with your company. This includes engagements that extend well beyond the purchasing touchpoints, such as social media engagements, online advertising, and customer service interactions. Therefore, by mapping these interactions, you can abstract valuable insights into what's working and - most importantly - what's not working for them.

- *How does each interaction influence the customer's perspective?*
- *What are your customer's needs and expectations?*
- *Which channels do your customers use the most?*
- *Are there any friction points across your customer's journey?*

Once you have mapped out the journey for each type of customer, you will have the answers to these questions to identify better the gaps between the desired and your current performance as a business and refocus efforts on new areas of your customer experience that could stand improvement.

2. Develop an Omni channel CX Strategy

An **Omni channel strategy** is extremely important for businesses to better understand their customers and their behaviour throughout their lifecycle. That's because, with an Omni channel CX strategy, you don't just meet your customers where they are - that's only the cherry on top. By providing a consistent multichannel communication journey for your customers, you go a step further and ensure that their conversation history and context follow them flawlessly across all channels. When it comes to delivering a good experience, **context** - like who your customer is, what emails they've opened, or what's in their shopping basket - is crucial.

Ultimately, an Omni channel CX strategy aims to provide a **cohesive customer experience** regardless of the channel (online or offline) through which your customers reach out to you. Here's what you can do to ensure a seamless customer journey:

- Make sure your website is mobile-friendly.
- Determine which channels your customers are using the most and choose to invest your time and marketing efforts there.
- Keep your content relevant to each marketing channel (for example, photos and videos do well on TikTok and Instagram, while longer text-based content works better on blog posts or newsletters).
- Provide cross-channel customer support, such as email support, social media messaging, or phone calls.
- Invest in online and offline marketing tools, like easy-to-use email marketing software for personalized campaigns, customizable website builders, social media management software, and in-store experiences for in-house clients.

3. Allow Customer Feedback to Lead the Way:

No matter how well you think you know your customers, there will always be some drivers, needs, or struggles in their journey that you won't be aware of - unless they *tell* you themselves.

Customer feedback is a very powerful tool if used properly. That's why the most successful companies base everything they do, from product creation to marketing initiatives, on the feedback they gather from their customers.

Feedback from customers can give insight into customers' expectations, as well as how they might change over time as your industry changes. Furthermore, you can discover where customers get stuck and what works well. Customer feedback is also the best way to pinpoint and acknowledge your business issues so you can do your best to address them. Moreover, listening to your customers and acting on their feedback helps build trust and reassure them that you value and respect their opinions.

Here are some of the most effective ways to **encourage and collect your customers' feedback**:

- Customer feedback surveys

- Email and customer contact forms
- Usability tests
- Customer interviews
- Social media platforms

4. Deliver Superior Customer Service

Customers choose to do business with you not just because your product or service meets their needs. They choose you repeatedly because they feel confident, they will receive the support they need when needed. A great service experience leads customers to **buy more and stay loyal to a brand for longer** and can be a powerful differentiator from your competitors.

In other words, **customer service** is the foundation of every great customer experience, and some data proves it:

- A whopping 91% of customers say good service makes them more likely to purchase from a company again. (*Salesforce*)
- 89% of businesses now compete on the level of service they deliver to customers rather than just on their products and services. (*Gartner*)

- Customers who think a company has good service are 38% more likely to recommend that company to their network.

Some **ways to improve your customer service** include:

- Having trained and supported employees to grow customer service skills and behaviours.
- Delivering on quality, not just on speed and efficiency.
- Running your business on flexible, scalable, and easy-to-use infrastructure.
- Offering multiple channels for support as part of your Omni channel approach.
- Optimizing delivery and response times.
- Use benchmark metrics like Net Promoter Score *(NPS)* to ensure you continually improve.

5. Personalise the Customer Journey

Personalization has always been in trend. However, today's customers seek more than personalized interactions; they demand them. According to *Accenture*, 1/3 of customers will abandon a brand if their experience isn't personalized enough.

Personalization allows the experience to adapt for each customer based on what you know about them and empowers you to deliver the right content at the right time to the right person. Delivering **personalized customer experiences** is the key to making customers feel valued and creating strong bonds between your brand and customers.

Depending on the scale and scope of your company, personalization can take on many forms, including:

- Sending personalized notes, gifts, or products to your customers.
- Offering loyalty schemes and money-off vouchers to your best buyers.
- Using data to personalize survey questions.
- Providing product recommendations based on past purchases or search history.
- Engaging with customers over their preferred contact method, account type, or status.
- Personalized online experiences, such as dynamic website content based on user preferences.
- Using geolocation technology to personalize your services based on location.

Creating **customer personas** and understanding your customers' preferences, personalities, habits, etc., can help you better target your personalization efforts. Additionally, UX research on your business's support initiatives can also be used to make customer interactions more personalized.

Note: Today, personalization is a digital transformation journey in which you can embark modestly (with automated personalized emails, for example) or deep dive right into AI- and data-driven personalization. The choice is yours, but you can't afford to miss the boat.

Picture Credit: www.google.com

6. Leverage the Power of Artificial Intelligence

According to *Gartner*, 70% of customer interactions today involve an emerging technology such as machine-learning applications, chatbots, or mobile messaging.

Industry-leading companies are quickly adapting by leveraging the power of emerging technologies like AI to improve customer experiences and achieve faster growth. For instance, more and more businesses are deploying **AI-powered chatbots** and virtual assistants to improve their customer service and increase engagement.

A chatbot can save businesses up to 30% on customer support costs, speed up response times, and answer up to 80% of FAQs. Moreover, bots are the best way to address customer requests in real-time and reduce customer frustrations from being on hold or queuing.

Other ways to **enhance CX with AI** tech include:

- Auto-responses to routine customer queries when your support team is busy or unavailable.
- Customer service interactions run by AI which give you time to focus on more complex issues.
- Customer base segmentation and increased personalization. By collecting user data from every touchpoint, AI can auto-send personalized messages and even track responses.

7. Invest in the Right Tech, Tools and People

According to an *Oracle* survey, 2/3 of companies today use at least one advanced technology for CX, and almost half of those who use AI reported increased sales per customer.

Undoubtedly, it's only easy to create breakthrough customer experiences in the digital era with the right technology and tools. From chatbots for customers around the clock to **natural language processing**, which allows you to understand free-form text messages, and **machine learning** that creates tailor-made CX experiences, the latest digital technology has made time-to-insights faster and personalization more scalable and affordable. And there's more:

- **Next-generation digital tools** allow you to engage customers across multiple channels and automate workflows.
- **Automated messages** help you increase customer engagement and deliver faster support.
- With **predictive analytics,** you can reduce churn and find solutions to complicated problems.
- **Customer data platforms (CDPs)** allow you to build unified customer profiles.

- With **testing and optimization tools**, you can get creative with your products.
- **Digital and voice assistants** provide new ways for customers to interact with you.
- **AI and related tech** allow you to offer more personalized interactions.

8. Virtual Metaverse Experiences

The metaverse will enable businesses to prioritize their consumers in a world where virtual selling will eventually become the standard by offering personalized involvement regardless of where the engagement occurs. Brands are learning how to create emotionally engaging customer experiences as the metaverse continues to grow. Although most metaverse worlds now exist in 2D, they'll soon be primarily virtual environments that may be accessed by VR, AR, and XR devices. The metaverse market is expected to reach $678.8 billion by 2030.

For CX, companies can create virtual environments where clients can interact with representatives and peers for a tailored shopping experience. Thanks to these online showrooms, customers may have a thorough grasp of the brand and product they're considering buying. 35% of people are prepared to shell out between $700 and $1,000 for VR gear that will give them the sensation of actually feeling what they experience in the metaverse.

For instance, the universe of NIKELAND was developed by apparel giant Nike. Users can create mini-games using interactive sports materials and the NIKELAND toolset while playing with online friends. Users in the online store may build their avatars with a virtual selection of Nike footwear, apparel, and accessories.

9. The Rise of Voice Technology

Voice technology will grow to $30 billion in 2026. Applications for voice recognition are nothing new, but AI-powered digital voice adds a degree of sophistication. To develop sophisticated applications that allow robots to connect with humans in a natural, conversational manner, natural language processing (NLP) and conversational AI are integrated with machine learning and natural language understanding (NLU).

A brand must invest in a solution specifically designed to manage human voice conversations to offer the most incredible experience to every voice touchpoint and every call for the modern customer, who demands empathy and personalization in every connection. Voice search statistics show that 58.6% of US-based consumers have tried using voice search. Many brands are using voice technology brilliantly.

For example, through the "Mercedes Me" connect voice app, Alexa can be used to remotely unlock doors, start the engine, control pre-conditioning, send a point of interest to your in-car navigation, locate the car, send an address, or access information about the vehicle, such as the amount of fuel it has left or its maintenance schedule. By leveraging voice AI, brands present a superior brand experience at scale.

10. Rising Focus on Privacy & Security

86% of consumers are concerned about data privacy, 78% fear the data collected, and 40% said they don't trust brands to use their data ethically. Concerns about data privacy are justified. Hence, 60% of the users want companies to be more transparent about their data use.

AI is currently used for many functions, including customer self-service bots, employee HR portals, virtual assistants, companion chatbots and robots, predictive analytics, and many other applications. With AI-driven methodologies to identify sensitive data throughout a data ecosystem in batch and real-time, businesses may speed up data privacy initiatives. The real-time use case is intriguing, particularly for companies searching for a solution to classify sensitive data and immediately apply a form of security like tokenization.

5.6 Implications of Customer Experience(CX)

61% *of customers are ready to switch to a competitor brand immediately after just one bad experience. But when there is more than one bad experience, the number magnifies to 80%.*

A single bad customer experience can damage a brand and ultimately impact its bottom line. Therefore, businesses are making all efforts to improve customer experience.

Brands have come to learn that customer experience matters in many ways:

- Increases revenues
- Strengthens brand preference
- Deepens customer loyalty
- Lowers costs by reducing customer churn

No doubt, customer experience is the new path to go.

And more so because - 73% of companies with above-average customer experience perform better financially than their competitors.

1. Your customers have demands.

They aren't what you think. Technologies and improvements that increase speed, convenience, friendliness, and knowledge—core demands of consumers—are openings for companies to improve how people interact with, embrace, and spend with their brands.

2. Customers generate revenue.

Employees drive the experience. Reduce friction for consumers and empower employees to drive customer satisfaction. This requires new working methods, a focus on employee experience, and a sophisticated view of human-and-machine relationships.

3. Technology can't solve experience problems.

It's only an enabler. Realign your priorities. Great employee experience leads to more robust, intelligent, and innovative ideas. These will drive future business and superb customer experience.

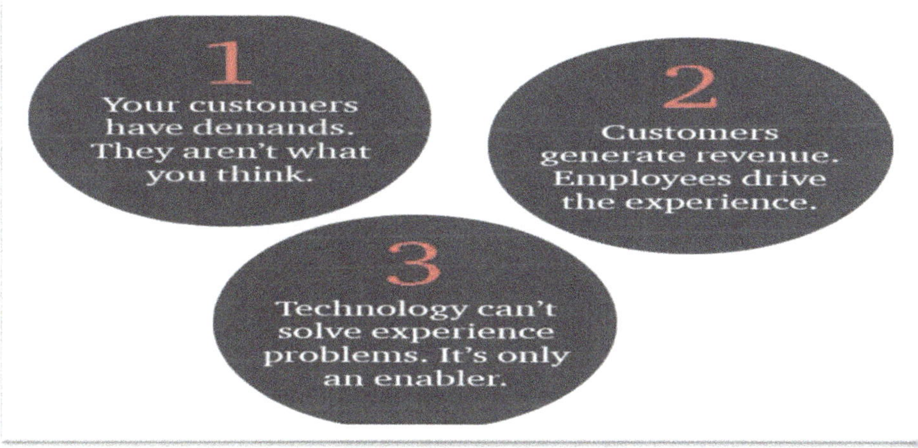

Picture Credit: www.google.com

How do we build the right CX strategy?

The most effective CX strategies describe how you want customers to feel and the experience you wish.

Picture Credit: www.google.com

A customer-first strategy is built from the top down. Management prioritizes customer needs and communicates those values to the rest of the organization. If everyone at the company is putting the customer first, then you'll have a culture that revolves around customer success and delight – not just the occasional interaction where a rep goes above and beyond.

A customer experience strategy is defined as a holistic plan to **increase customer satisfaction** and engagement across all interactions with your brand, from discovery to post-purchase

The hard truth is that there is no universal customer experience strategy, any more than there is a single brand or business strategy that works for all. When it comes to developing the right strategy, these are four of the best-practice activities common to CX leaders:

- **Change company culture to be more customer-centric:** Weaving culture into CX activities is key, in no small part because to accomplish this you'll need to determine what customer centricity means to you, then communicate to all across the org.
- **Align brand and CX strategies:** Recognizing that your brand sets very real expectations of what your customers can expect, it's crucial to crisply align your brand and CX strategies to ensure you're organized to keep the promises you're making.
- **Assign a dedicated customer experience executive:** Getting organizational buy-in is a significant challenge, and crucial to the success of your efforts. The right executive will lead, influence, and educate, communicating the vision and bringing the broader organization along.

- **Formally align business and CX strategies:** Just as your brand and CX strategies align, they both need to ladder back to business strategy. For example, if you compete on innovation, this leads to a different posture for, and expectations of, CX than if you compete on value or customer intimacy.

Your customer experience strategy needs to reflect your unique business, brand, and vision for the future. Aligning these things in ways that inform, guide, and inspire your people and provide a clear path forward is both a challenge and an opportunity.

Let's see how to build a strategy for customer experience

"In a world where products and services are becoming more and more commoditized, customer experience is the only true differentiator." By Annette Franz

1. Understand your audience and create buyer personas

Understand your customers. Who are they? What are their motivations? This information will allow you to build customer personas that you'll later use to shape your strategy.

For example, categorize the types of customers your customer support team speaks with and note their needs. Also, collect data from your CRM or customer experience management platform.

Once you have enough information, create buyer personas and use them in marketing campaigns.

2. Analyse your business objectives

What are your business goals? New customers? Entering a new market?

Perhaps you are launching **products or services** into a current marketplace. Review brand studies and identify the barriers. How can they be overcome?

Ask yourself: how can your customer experience strategy framework help you achieve your **long-term goals**?

3. Reverse-engineer the experience you want to deliver

Steve Jobs was an advocate of "beginning with the customer experience and working backward to the technology". This approach could work for your company, too.

For example, you can start by listing your brand's customer experience stages. Where are the opportunities to make an impression? (For Amazon, for example, it's early delivery.) Start from there and ask: what do we need to make sure customers go through this stage seamlessly?

4. Hire team players and get them invested in the process

Employees are key to **delivering great customer experience**. Damien Peillon, from Logo Genie, trains employees to pay attention to customers. If a customer mentions a birthday when making a reservation, the manager will come over to wish them well at the table.

What can we learn from this? Hire people who have a customer experience mindset, even if they're not in customer-facing roles. Then, pay attention to the details. Knowing customer likes and dislikes gives the chance to act on them, personalizing the experience.

5. Eliminate bad design early in the game

User experience (UX) is key when it comes to **creating a customer experience strategy**. That's because UX design is essential for the main points where customers enter their relationship with your brand, namely your product and/or your website.

Three design tips to **improve customer experience**:

- Create a consistent brand experience across channels - your website, apps, email, and **social media channels**. Take inspiration from Etsy's orange and white theme.
- Eliminate unnecessary hurdles and streamline the process of purchasing. Make it easy to find the right information or service.
- The Emotion factor: Wufoo included emoji faces in their app, ranging from super smiley to mega grumpy. Customers were asked to rate how they were feeling based on this scale.

6. Pay attention to customer feedback

According to research from Bain & Company, 80 percent of companies believe they are providing great customer service, but only eight percent of customers agree with them.

Asking for **customer feedback** is the best way to close this gap. Here's how:

- Use post-interaction and **real-time** feedback surveys. Follow up with customers over the phone or email to get clarifications.
- Practice social listening. Social media is where customers are usually the most honest and vocal.

7. Research your competitors

Analyse competitors and market trends to get a clear picture. What are they doing to service your target audience?

Sometimes you can play catchup with what your competitors are doing to avoid being left behind. Other times, you can identify gaps, such as CX tactics no one is using.

8. Build systems for quick and effective resolutions

Customer support can be the pillar of your **customer experience strategy plan**. There's nothing more frustrating than looking for a solution to a problem and not having a clear and fast way to get it.

Thankfully, there are a lot of tech options that can help you build an effective support process. For example, **live chat** is super convenient for customers browsing your website. It's easy to access when needed without being distracting. It can be integrated with video chat and chatbots for even higher-quality support.

9. Incorporate a memorable brand personality

A unique brand personality can result in a massive, loyal **customer base**. Apple, Amazon, Target, and many other companies are trusted to provide memorable experiences to their customers because they build their brands around them.

Create a unified brand identity by getting feedback from your **employee experience**, analysing the market, and brainstorming ideas about what your business wants to be for your customers.

10. Apply AI technology

More than 6 out of 10 U.S. customers prefer a digital self-service tool (website, mobile app, or online tutorial) over a call or video chat for resolving issues. This experience can be enhanced by AI tech.

Here are some benefits of AI:

- Enable auto-responses to routine customer queries, guiding your audiences with carefully curated content.
- Customer service interactions run by AI reduce the need to attend every customer conversation, freeing up your agents to focus on more complex issues.

11. Understand your customer experience metrics and Optimize

Failing to **measure your customer experience** means missing out on valuable information that can boost your customer experience strategy. Remember, if it can't be measured, it can't be improved.

A customer experience strategy is an ongoing process. Adopt a continuous improvement approach. Measure, optimize, repeat.

Remember: customer experience provides a massive opportunity to **boost customer loyalty**. With the right strategy in place, the sky's the limit.

12. Make use of the right technology and tools

In the era of digital customer experience, no customer experience strategy would be possible without the right technology. With a robust customer experience platform, for example, you can:

- Engage customers across multiple channels all in one place.
- **Increase customer engagement** with automated messages and faster support.
- Reduce churn with predictive analytics.
- Personalize interactions.

5.7 Customer Experience (CX) strategy and Potential Opportunity

1. Listen to your customers. We're not talking about satisfaction surveys or asking "the ultimate question" to track a Net Promoter score–though this can be part of the equation. The issue with these solutions is that they don't point toward the problems or delights that drive those scores.

Listening to your customers means asking them what they think–and why. Then acting on it. Look at your VoC Program and ask yourself if a) it's collecting the information you need from the folks who count, and b) you're acting on what you hear and learn!

2. Remember: Customer perception *is* reality. The quality of your customer experience lives in one place: the mind of your customer. No matter how well you think you're doing, the gap between customer expectations of experience and their perceptions of experience is the reality you need to understand and address.

3. Make your customers part of the solution. Involving customers in the experience design process—experiences, services, products, even physical environments—has been around for a long time. It boils down to this: Take your customers' points of view into account before you start making decisions about what they might want or need!

4. Map your customer's journey. A customer journey map allows you to "walk in your customers' shoes" by traveling with them as they interact with your company. Research-based and focused on desired outcomes from the customer's perspective, you'll see what their needs are at each lifecycle stage and point of interaction, how well you meet/exceed/fall short of their expectations, and where opportunities for improvement lie.

5. Monitor customer interactions. Customer listening is just that: listening. Monitoring is critical, as well, because only you know all your touchpoints. Pulsed, planned, or transactional surveys, call-canter logs, complaint lines, Web feedback, and social media commentary—monitor your performance in all of these places, and more. Set KPIs based on customers' expectations and your planned experience, and monitor to see how well you do.

6. Get your data together. Most established companies keep customer data in silos across the enterprise: sales data in one bucket, marketing data in another; product and service somewhere else, and digital data in another entirely. All of this customer data needs to be integrated and easily accessible across your organization, so employees can truly "see" the relationship between you and your customer, and make decisions as a result. This is one of the greatest challenges faced by companies and one of the most important to solve.

7. "See" your customers digitally. Every transaction between your company and your customers generates data about that transaction. Each online or mobile interaction generates "digital data trails" that can be stored and analysed. Looking at your customers through the lens of your digital relationship will provide valuable insights into behaviour that can help you radically improve customer experience.

8. Define your customer experience strategy. Customer experience strategy flows from your company's business and brand strategy. Just as brand strategy creates (and manages) customer expectations of a brand, your customer experience strategy is your plan to meet or exceed those expectations. With implications for virtually every aspect of your company, it's the vehicle through which you can turn customer expectations into reality.

9. Empower and reward your employees. In the quest to be more customer-centric, your employees are the frontline. They boast a wealth of insight about customers and internal operations, and can quickly improve customer experience through one-on-one interactions and behind-the-scenes decision-making. Yet many companies have reward structures tied only to revenue, versus meeting the needs of customers. They don't empower employees to make the decisions required to meet those customer needs.

Now that you've read this list, where can you take advantage of these opportunities in your own company? And what further ideas can you add to this list? Keep this in mind: The secret to customer-centricity is based on designing your world around an understanding of your customer's needs and a focus on actually meeting those needs.

This core idea relates to everything on this list—and should relate to everything in yours.

5.8 Becoming A Customer Company

"If you do build a great experience, customers tell each other about that. Word of mouth is very powerful. "

According to a recent Harvard Business Review (HBR), organizations worldwide prioritize customer experience (CX). To deliver an experience that customers value, you have to 1) know them, 2) organize around their unique expectations throughout their journey, and 3) serve them personally and in real-time.

HBR found that only 16% of CX-driven companies have a single (360-degree) view of customers. Even so, they need the organizational structure to use those insights. It's one thing to say you're "customer-centered," but it's entirely different when your company is organized around the customer.

As customer expectations and behaviours evolve along with times, trends, tastes, and technologies, CX becomes intrinsic to business success. When you consider how the customer experiences your company, what are their key touch points in doing business with you? They usually reside in marketing, commerce, and customer service. Most often, those functions, along with corresponding customer data, operate independently. As a result, the customer's experience is disconnected by design.

Research shows that 60% of customers feel like they're not communicating with one company, and 66% say they must repeat or re-explain information to different representatives. Separate research found that 85% of customers expect consistent interactions across departments.

It's indicators like this that point to customers who could be one step away from leaving your brand. 71% reported switching brands in the last year.

In an era of economic uncertainty, investing in the customer's experience–referring to it in the possessive form reminds us that their experience with our company is theirs–becomes a critical business growth engine. The better customers are served in each touch point and across their journey, the more likely they are to stay loyal. As an example, it was found that 94% of customers said that positive customer service experiences make them more likely to re-purchase.

Customer's Experience Transformation

Customer companies realize that internal value creation is a derivative of external value creation. The better you treat your customers, the more likely you are to retain them, the more likely they are to return, and, of course, the more likely they are to spread the word. Commerce is about community, and community is about relationships. Community used to be defined as social dealings between people. That's the core of a customer company.

Companies that connect the dots across every customer touch point through operations, technology, data, people, and processes will define the new blueprint for what it means to be a "customer company." This transformation starts with someone taking ownership and accountability of the entire customer journey, orchestrating and elevating the experience, and uniting the organization (and real-time data) around a future vision and motivating state of what customer-centricity looks and feels like.

"Customers will shape your success if you listen to them." Similarly, your failure will be shaped by customers if you don't listen to them.

With every strategic decision you make about the technology that powers service, commerce, and marketing, every decision about how you market, sell, and serve, remember, you are not your customer. How they experience your business counts for everything, and they must be involved in your decision rationale.

How to Achieve Customer Company Dream

1: Establish an "Office of the Customer" with representatives from key business groups

CMOs must partner with business leaders representing the touchpoints that define the customer's experience, including commerce, sales, and service. This team must also include leaders, including CIOs, CxOs, CFOs, and COOs, to support and facilitate rapid transformation. This group will serve as a cross-functional steering committee to bridge silos, establish governance, collaborate, and accelerate decision-making and experimentation.

More so, a sub-committee should be formed to serve as a centre of excellence to centralize the **voice of the customer** and coordinate best practices for integrated experience design and customer relationship management.

2: Experience the customer's experience

All executives can benefit from customer empathy and the ability to understand and share the feelings of their customers. This means that business leaders, i.e. decision-makers, must experience the customer's experience at each touch point. We want executives to feel the friction and frustration of doing business with their own company. We want executives to spend time with customers to hear from them what they love and don't love. The process should formally analyse and document the experience in every step and identify areas for improvement, gaps, and opportunities. Additionally, this is a chance to compare and contrast your brand and service promises and what customers experience.

3: Organize around real-time customer 360 data and insights

Place real-time insights at the canter of the business and the customer's experience. The only way to deliver a unified customer experience is for marketers to have a real-time 360 view and understanding of each customer. Integrate data from every step of the customer experience and create an automated, intelligent, and real-time customer profile record.

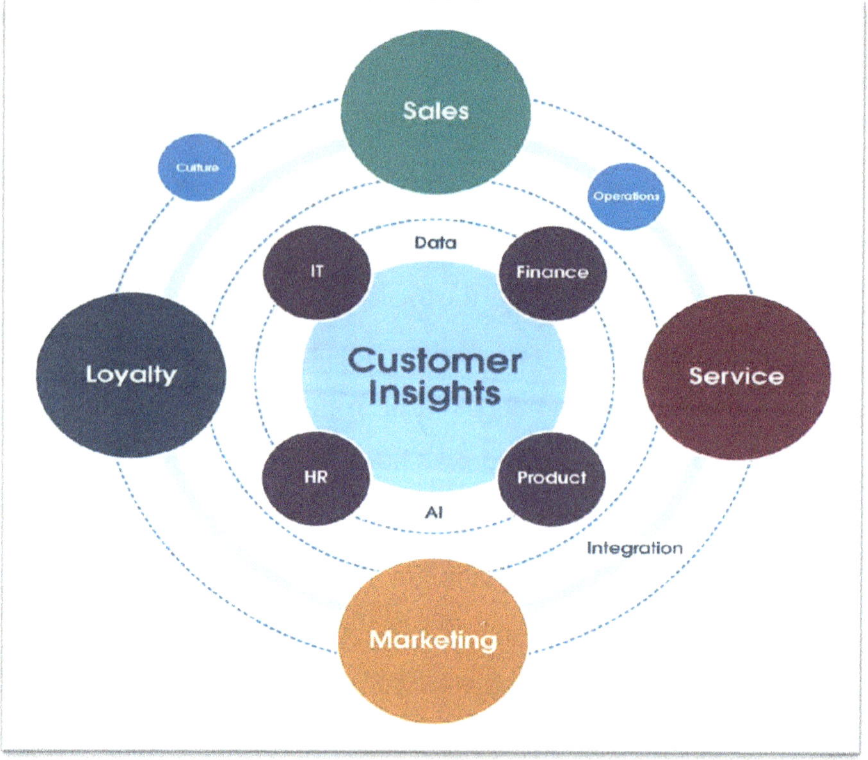

Picture Credit: www.google.com

4: Cultivate a 360 customer-unified data culture

With real-time customer data and insights at the canter of CX and operational transformation, leaders need to create a data culture that helps employees get closer to their customers.

Train and educate your employees on digital-first customer and data proficiency. Facilitate access to trusted real-time data sources across the customer's journey, making it easy for customer-facing employees to find relevant information. Collaborate with the centre Of excellence to cultivate data expertise and promote the voice of the customer. Define customer feedback loops and connect them to touchpoint leaders to deliver real-time, personalized, interconnected customer experiences.

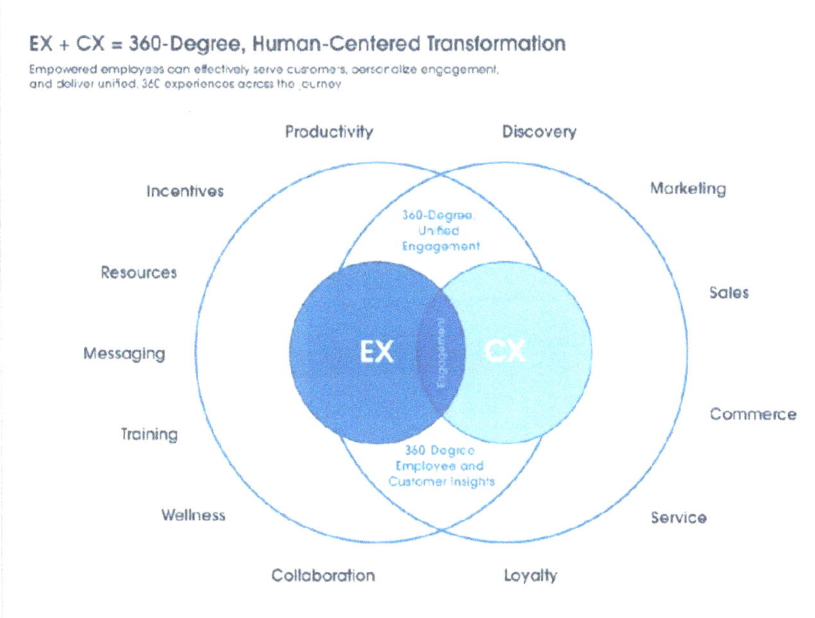

Picture Credit: www.google.com

5: Connect CX functions to a 360-degree CRM platform

Delivering personalized, real-time, and integrated experiences requires a connected, real-time platform that connects the touch points that shape the customer's experience.

Leading organizations are already uniting teams around a common CRM platform. 63% of elite marketers report using the same CRM system as sales and service departments. And 83% of service organizations use the same CRM system as their marketing and sales colleagues.

AI is also helping companies to personalize engagement with the proper context to make messaging, next best action, and recommendations more accurate and relevant. For example, 64% of high-performing organizations automatically suppress marketing when a service case opens.

6: Design the experience you want customers to have, share, and recall

In the same way, marketing-savvy companies operate with a brand style guide; the same should be true for CX. Start by defining your signature experience and ensure that it aligns with the brand and service promise. Everything should be connected and complementary. This vision becomes your motivator for a future state, serving as the sheet music for cross-functional teams supported by technologies, processes, and policies.

Identify the touchpoints, processes, skills/training, and systems gaps your organization needs to deliver against an upgraded vision. Think of this as an aspirational customer journey map, not just improving the journey as it exists. Treat it like a template for future state experiences you want customers to have.

7: Connect the dots across the customer journey

Every company must build an integrated omnichannel, mobile, and edge journey. A whopping 70% of organizations fail to connect user experiences ultimately, and 55% say it's difficult to integrate those user experiences.

Organizations report that 72% of customer interactions are now digital, according to a recent MuleSoft study. Marketers state that "creating a cohesive customer journey across channels and devices" is both a top priority and a challenge.

But the results are compelling for those CX leaders who do connect the dots for customers. In its research, MuleSoft learned that of the organizations integrating customer experiences, 54% see a lift in customer engagement, 50% increase innovation (50%), and 48% improve ROI.

8: Reimagine the roles of marketing and service in the 360 customer journey

The relationship between marketing and service are bookends in CX. They require reimagination and innovation to deliver customers a personalized, real-time, end-to-end journey.

Engage customers before the time of need. Employ AI to reimagine the idea of reactive service. Introduce proactive, predictive, and preventative engagement opportunities that help customers before they require help or personalize their experiences during their lifecycles.

Make automated engagement conversational. Use automation and user experience design to make IVR, chatbot, and self-service decision trees and processes intuitive, efficient, conversational, and enjoyable. Better yet, consider conversational AI and digital humans to bring automated touchpoints to life as if they were powered by Alexa, Siri, or, better yet, Jarvis from Iron Man!

Empower reps to personalize engagement. Free-up agents to be more creative beyond traditional scripts.

· Employ AI to provide real-time personalization, call coaching, and next-best action and experience. Offer live, video-based engagement for product overviews, shopping services, support, and workshops.

· Introduce co-browsing technology or group/social shopping capabilities to facilitate multiple experiences at the same time.

· Reskill agents to augment chatbots and conversational AI to help customers in the discovery and search phase make decisions on purchases when technology reaches its limits.

Transform field services into a service and loyalty asset: Field services represent one of the most promising and immediate opportunities for innovation and growth, with the traditional four-hour appointment window unacceptable for today's consumers. And it's setting the stage for an appointment economy. Appointment-setting helps businesses be more thoughtful about field service, plan more effectively, use resources more efficiently, and aim to deliver a higher quality in-person service. Doing so values the customer's time and presence to deliver outcomes that benefit everyone.

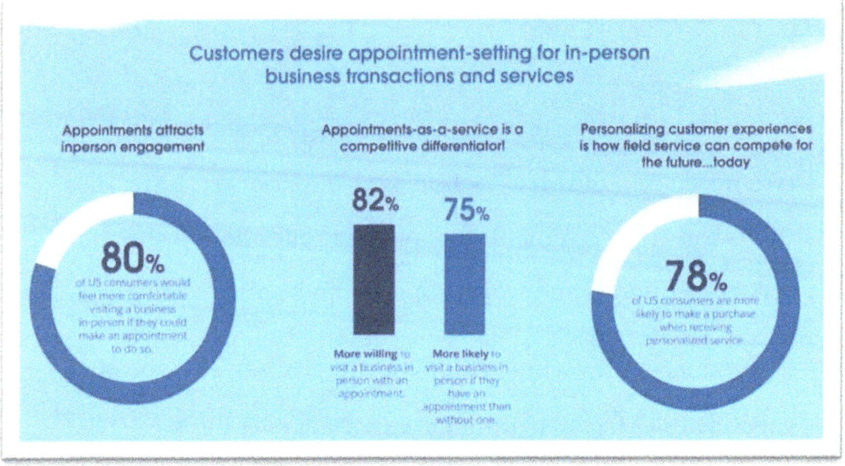

Picture Credit: www.google.com

The advantages of appointment-setting in field service

SALESFORCE

Post-Commerce Service. Post-purchase customer engagement represents under-utilized touchpoints for relationship- and loyalty-building. Following each transaction, businesses create opportunities to connect further (gather relevant data), personalize engagement, and enhance customer retention. Beyond general surveys, post-commerce services can offer guidance and communities for product experiences, prompt collaboration opportunities, and pre-emptive support.

Redesign the mobile customer journey. Mobile-first journeys should be designed for their unique form factors, operating systems, and platforms. For example, web pages that are adapted to mobile screens aren't innate to mobile gestures. Think more like the user interfaces of TikTok, Snapchat, and Bumble.

In another example, QR code adoption skyrocketed by 750%, but rather than reimagine mobile-first experiences that came to life on mobile screens, and links often opened static web pages. What if they unlocked augmented reality or 3D objects, immersive experiences, games, or media? Even though you may already have a branded app, customers seek to go through the entire journey via native user experiences and user interfaces, not those adapted from the traditional web. Apps, too, should take design cues from the best apps in the game, particularly those outside your industry.

9: Upgrade metrics to measure 360 customer experiences, business transformation, and growth.

In addition to capturing important engagement metrics in each touch point, businesses must also measure the customer's experience across their journey. This means silos have to collaborate. For example, 81% of marketing teams are learning to share goals and metrics with sales. Eighty percent of marketers are also doing so with service and commerce. And roughly half (48%) of marketing organizations today track important experience metrics such as customer lifetime value (CLV/LTV).

In service and support, customer effort emerged as a crucial metric to measure the time and steps customers take to get a resolution. A lower customer effort score can lead to increased customer satisfaction. This methodology could also be applied to the journey itself. Consider developing a customer experience performance indicator (CXPI) that measures connectedness, personal engagement, and delight, i.e. do customers feel like their journey is integrated, personalized, and delightful?

Conclusion:

You can't just say you are customer-centric or that you're now, automagically, a customer company. It takes more than words and clever marketing. Customers not only see through it, they feel it. Your investments in the customer's experience are reflective of your commitment to becoming truly customer-focused, cantered, and obsessed, however, you may describe it.

In times of disruption, and honestly, at any time, focusing on customer acquisition isn't enough to grow, and certainly not what it takes to thrive as a customer company.

Your customers need to know you know them. Investing in customer retention is the key to profitable growth. And it's harder than ever to engage and retain customers. The only way to achieve sustainable growth is through relevance, which means you must know your customers and become your customers.

In this digital- and mobile-first and real-time, uncertain world, every company must rethink the customer's experience as the blueprint for transformation and innovation. Let go of pre-2020 mindsets, processes, and investments that don't track toward customer relevance or future trends. Let go of sunken cost bias. Instead, dive in, at whatever pace and capacity you can, to explore how to reimagine and lead the next era of the customer's experience.

The CXO's Journey

"Quality in a service or product is not what you put into it. It is what the customer gets out of it."

Today, CIOs part of the CXO journey work very closely with the CXO team. The journey from traditional to transformational for CXOs represents a profound shift in how organizations prioritize and approach the customer experience (CX). Real-World Examples of CXO Transformation To illustrate the real-world impact of CXO transformation, let's examine two notable examples:

1. Amazon: A Customer-Centric Giant

Amazon's success is primarily due to its relentless focus on the customer experience. Founder Jeff Bezos famously left an empty chair in meetings to symbolize the customer's presence. Amazon's CXO transformation involves leveraging data to personalize recommendations, offering a seamless shopping experience, and prioritizing customer satisfaction.

2. Disney: Creating Magical Experiences

Disney has a long history of prioritizing the customer experience. Their CXO transformation involves integrating technology, such as MagicBands and mobile apps, to enhance the visitor experience in their theme parks. Disney's commitment to storytelling and attention to detail creates memorable moments that keep customers returning.

Looking Ahead: The Future of CXO Transformation

As we peer into the future, CXO's transformation will continue to evolve in response to changing customer expectations and technological advancements. Here are some trends and predictions that will shape the future of CXOs:

1. AI-Powered Personalization

Artificial intelligence and machine learning will play an increasingly prominent role in tailoring customer experiences. AI will analyse vast amounts of data to provide hyper-personalised recommendations and solutions.

2. Ethical Customer Engagement

Customers are becoming more conscious of ethical and social issues. CXOs will need to ensure that their customer engagement strategies align with these values and address sustainability, inclusivity, and other ethical concerns.

3. Seamless Omni channel Experiences

Customers expect seamless transitions between online and offline channels. CXOs will focus on integrating technology to provide consistent experiences across all touchpoints.

4. Data Privacy and Security

As data collection becomes more extensive, protecting customer data will be paramount. CXOs must implement robust data privacy and security measures to build customer trust.

5. Customer-First Culture

CXO's transformation will extend beyond the C-suite to create a customer-centric culture throughout the organization. Every employee will understand their role in delivering exceptional experiences.

REFERENCE:

- State of the CIO Survey 2023 Report
- Harvard Business Review (HBR) Report by Sales Force
- Google.com (all the images used are Google free images by Google search) and links are published for public consumption)
- www.cio.com
- https://www.michaelpage.at/
- https://www.linkedin.com/
- https://www.ciowatercooler.co.uk/
- https://www.cxotalk.com/
- Author's Articles which are published and available in Google for free search
- https://www.ciodialogues.com/index.php/cio-voice/fail-fast-first-time-right/
- https://cionews.co.in/i-always-try-to-keep-my-technology-skills-up-to-date/
- https://www.ciodialogues.com/index.php/thought-leadership/meet-your-customer-expectation-with-fail-fast-approach/
- http://www.acceptmission.com/